TORTURING THE
VILLAGERS

TORTURING THE VILLAGERS

STEVEN FRANSSEN

stevenfranssen.com

twitter.com/stevefranssen

youtube.com/c/stevenfranssen

To the jokers.

Preface

This book has no table of contents. It was written in almost exactly six weeks. There is no Book One, Book Two, etc. My more longstanding readers will recognize the style as similar to *Make Self-Knowledge Great Again*. This book has a broader focus than one subject alone. The cover probably sums it up well, though I disavow the use of cigarettes. That's in there for the mood. I disavow premarital sex, as an aside.

Our guys need some kino content, something that will stimulate us and make us laugh. That's the spirit of this book. It contains universally applicable principles that any person can benefit from. But this isn't so much a book for women or *others*. This is for our guys. If you're not one of our guys, you won't *get it*. Not used to exclusivism, eh? Nor am I. Let's see what we can get into here.

-Steven Franssen
October, 2019

Physiognomy and Constitutional Psychology

"Physiognomy and constitutional psychology are completely legitimate— I don't believe for one second that it's not significant that Charlie Kirk and David Hogg are nefarious political actors and they look the way they do. David Hogg is ghoulish because he is a bad faith actor, same with Charlie Kirk. (Good thread here by Steve expanding on physiognomy)." -Nick Fuentes; Sept. 2019

I'm a Western man. If you don't dress like a Western man and wear that spirit in you, you're an echo of some clothing factory in China or Indonesia.

If you're Western, embrace it in your appearance. But we're not talking about "clothing style" here. That's weird and gay.

We're talking about how you are in your essence. Physiognomy and constitutional psychology. Your physique is the physical manifestation of your will, more or less. Don't think this automatically means more muscles = more power. And the AURA you exude is entirely your responsibility.

The Bible is full of examples of men with intense personal, Western auras. And so was our lore before the *white liberals* consolidated all the publication and distribution companies within the first 20-30 years of arriving to America.

Go read about Teddy Roosevelt or Winston Churchill's early years. Learn about Orson Welles' childhood. Or try to understand Douglas MacArthur or George S. Patton. These men were fundamentally Western. They had an edge, the likes of which I won't describe publicly, that exuded in their auras. They were primal. And it bore in their appearances. I'm sure you can think of a few other men like this (wink, wink).

Ezra Pound, Howard Taft, Charles Lindbergh, a few "men against time" that have arisen and fallen.

Do you carry yourself this way or are you a burden to yourself? Does the outgroup fear you or are you submissive, wearing logos that brand you as a consumer, and keeping your eyes glued to a cell phone that records everything you say and is always watching you for certain keywords.

Charlie Kirk is a ghoul because he bears a spiritual brand on him, like you would take a branding iron to your cattle. Same with David Hogg.

I don't bear that brand. And I am unendingly "unhappy" at seeing how many around me are openly accepting their branding. Yes, very "unhappy" about it.

Some modern-day dudes who exude "it" well:

-Alex Jones

-Trump (there's even a word "Trumpian")

-Pepe the Frog

-Jared Taylor

-Ann Coulter

One of the dangers of Hollywood is that it acts as this talent-suck wherein SOME people who would be distinguished in their physiognomy because of their WESTERN spiritual depth are instead wholly and completely retrained to put that energy into the service of Satan/fiat/power/etc.

We see bizarro representations of what it means to be us, but in a fundamentally unsubversive way. Since we're mirroring, empathizing creatures - we become less and less of ourselves.

There have only been very, very few to pierce this veil out of sheer talent. Mel Gibson is one. There are probably a few others. Tom Selleck when he was young. Maybe even Kevin Sorbo (Liam Neeson is a better guess), Bruce Willis, and Nick Nolte (if I'm really reaching). But these guys won't take it up the ass as has been required since around 9/11 and so they've been doing side studio or self-funded work ever since. Or they took it up the ass, like Russell Crowe did, and now they're soft and self-hating.

This is the power of imagery. Of iconography. We used to get all this input from Church and from realist art. But even those were perverted.

Andrew Jackson. Go read the actual things he said (not the faggy psyop that the neocons have been doing on him). Now imagine his deeds. Now imagine being with him in-person. George Washington was the same way. Other people whose speeches you're not supposed to read were this way.

Put it together. Weigh the words and actions and then figure out the "aura". Choose the very best.

Consider this in the light of your being conditioned to embody Brad Pitt, who is in TWO super major tentpole releases in 2019. Only The Rock gets bigger play than that. These men ACT like they take it up the ass and they LOVE it.

This is Satanic. You're being programmed. These are the icons set forth.

Read old books and watch old footage instead.

If it's true that they make every colonel and every special-ops team guy do some weird ritual to make it, consider how weird and queer Dan Crenshaw is despite this tremendous pedigree he has that a hundred and fifty years ago would have made him a lion. Notice all the high-level vets out there who keep extremely to themselves and won't signal their participation in the armed forces like the low-level ones do.

Personally, I want to have more in common with young Ernest Hemmingway (before he drank away his talent) or Keiser Wilhelm than I do with Charlie Kirk, David Hogg, Joe Biden, Obama, The Rock, Leo DiCaprio, Tom Hanks, LeBron James, etc.

These men feel like a queer, alien species to me. They don't feel Western in the slightest. I have no trust in them. Their body language is disgusting to me. Foul and alien.

Only the physiognomy of subversive, true Westerners should ever be emulated. And it has to be found deep within or passed down through parenting from fathers who never allowed the brand on themselves. Or found in books and divined accordingly by highly aware young men who are unmarked.

Think about this. I don't give a damn if it makes you uncomfortable or if you think I sound paranoid.

Be a man. Not the faggot they're psyoping you to be. Notice how we're all being neurologically programmed away from our hearts and toward our anuses.

Stay Sharp

Red flag phrases in women's dating profiles:

-dog mom

-"single mom"

-love to travel

-check out brew pubs

-"anti-Trump"

s-sarcastic

-"drama free"

-yoga lover

-down-to-earth

-vegan/feminist

-love sports

Someone asks me: Why 'down to earth' though?

I respond: Usually means she's not high IQ. Can also mean "submissive to the point of self-erasing".

Someone else asks me: Why 'love to travel'?

I respond: Usually means they're brainwashed by radical egalitarianism, consumerism, and multiculturalism. Indicates they lack an inner life, are estranged from Christianity/their families, and that they lack the capacity to think beyond what they were spoon fed in public school.

I sat next to a woman on a plane recently. She immediately made "fuck me" eyes at me when I indicated to her that I would be sitting next to her. Her sexual aggression surprised me. I live on a small acreage somewhere semi-rural with a virtuous woman and a couple of big dogs. I've been with this woman for a decade, before third wave feminism really took off. Not used to the "our world is dying we may as well fuck each other to whittle away the time" culture that originates in San Francisco and Manhattan, ejaculating itself constantly into the heartland. Probably via plane! Perhaps we should ban airline travel altogether.

That gets me thinking about the film *Witness* starring Harrison Ford. Go look up the synopsis. I'm not going to write it here. The whole series of events plays out the way it does because an Amish woman decides to take her son via train travel to visit a family member in another place, much too far to go by horse and buggy as is their custom. Had they not got on that train, that boy would have never witnessed a murder. Harrison Ford's detective character would have never come to Amish country to hide out, presumably fucking the woman one night in a brief scene that breaks their tension. She wouldn't have shown her breasts to him when she caught him looking. None of this degenerate, Boomer crap would have happened. Hell, he even dances to some bland Motown song with her in her barn when he gets the power to his car going again. Don't get me started on the dance scene from *Frantic*. Go look it up. Cringiest scene from cinema of all time. I felt like I was drunk off of cheap Chinese wine. At the time, I probably was. Long time ago. No more of that.

Back to this woman on the plane. She looked at me again when I sat down. Lady, take it easy! I'm here to fly home and see my innocent child and tender wife.

FUCK ME
FUCK ME
FUCK ME

That was her constant refrain. She had nice legs. Not bad looking, either. Just a little used up. She'd been doing this too long. Probably three years out of college. She hasn't given college up. She needed constant amusement. While our plane was taxiing forever to take off, she watched the Titans play the…oh, I don't remember. Football. The most globo-homo sport there is. Golf is probably the most respectable. When the Wi-Fi ran out and we were in the air, she rubbed her smooth leg up against me "accidentally". Easy, lady! She had on short shorts and a hoodless sweatshirt from her alma mater. Nice legs, I'll give her that much. She knows her assets. She proceeded to put on some Justin Timberlake movie where he's seducing some woman or something. The smarter one of the two from Good Will Hunting is in it. I forget his name. He was in some Netflix movie where they steal a bunch of money from a drug lord and then give it to his Hispanic daughter out of white guilt after he dies. Stupid bullshit. I click through these movies in about 15 minutes to keep my finger on the pulse of what people are taking in. It's getting so bad that I can't even do that anymore. *Hobbs and Shaw* is gay, anti-white porn. *Captain Marvel* is a spring-loaded walnut cracker around the testicles of a gym bro. *Men In Black International* is just chimpanzee feces thrown onto a mannequin of Tommy Lee Jones.

She's got this movie on and is shifting around uncomfortably. Can't tell if she's getting wet or it's indigestion. Yup, she farts real bad. I put my trusty old cap over my nose. I don't even try to hide it. Why hide anything from people out in the world? Just let her see that I smelled her rancid fucking fart and that I thoroughly disapprove. I know it was her. Flight attendants pass by with the four-hundred-pound cart and she loads up on wine. She spends sixteen bucks to get it. You know how many bags of hazelnuts I can buy for sixteen bucks? At least a couple. The wine seems to loosen up her bowels from whatever god-forsaken pub lunch tripe she put into it. She rips another bad fart. Time for poopie. She gets up like, "This isn't over yet!" I'm trying to hold on to the memories of a trip full of goodness and graciousness. Everyone around me is a Boomer or a psychotic liberal. The physiognomy doesn't lie. She gets back from her poopie, making fuck-me eyes at me again. At this point I want to throw up. She's not bad looking at all, either. Most men would be happy to wed her, put her in ankle length skirts, and watch her gather eggs from the chicken coop while she's holding a baby or two.

The stewardess also made fuck-me eyes at me after I checked her out because I'm programmed like an idiot to like her witchy, Kardashian aura. I snapped out of it after she did that because putting it in her would be like putting your cock into a Sarlacc Pit. You're mauled forever after something like that. At least your circumcision was probably forced on you. You have only yourself to blame for getting spiritual AIDS.

College girl next to me passes out from the wine. I feel relieved. She held no power over me. I'm just used to sitting in a leather chair, talking to geniuses over Skype, and looking out my window now and then to admire the mountains. She gave up the chase out of sheer emotional bloatedness. Probably owns a snuggie at home.

The stewardess was "higher caliber" and realized it was going to go nowhere with me after she sent out her initial ping in response to what was basically shock from me that there are actually people out in the world who do themselves up like she did. She was spurned and furious. She proceeded to flirt with a 20-year old, tall black dude for the better part of five minutes instead of doing her job. You whore. Same feeling I get when, well, that would get me in trouble so I'm not going to say it. Everyone wants to tattle on everyone else these days. Even Chapelle is saying it, to people's faces. I love it. The stewardess had some dark voodoo on her. She had a script tattoo down the inside of her arm on the bicep. Pure pre-Christian Kardashian. Pure witchcraft. The proverbial legs of the West spread wide open for the intrusion of the primordial hordes. She has a bad mark on her. She's a slave to sex. Eight out of ten with makeup. Seven without. Right in the "porn star sweet spot".

Maybe nobody's talked to you about this. The people who control the media and who run the major porn studios are only able to attain a certain level of "talent" when it comes to the women. Women past a certain quality of appearance are swept up by talent scouts for high fashion, which pays a *bit* better but comes with more prestige. Don't think those high fashion girls aren't passed around like trays of hors d'oeuvres at certain parties. There are thousands of people across the West whose only job is to find attractive women, above about an 8.5. Usually they're gunning for above a 9, though. I don't know exactly how it works but I know it has a strong hold in our economy. The women who do not meet this mark do not get the same kind of attention. They usually get married young to guys who can pull in bank. I'm talking about the 7.5's to about 8.5's. Below this threshold are the women who are recruited into porn. They're pretty enough to do a bit of modeling. Maybe some bridal shows. The porn recruiters spot their "fuckability" and entice them to strip and pose for pictures, each set riskier than the previous. Then, I don't know how it works from here because the only reliable documentaries that exist on the subject are on what women do *after* porn. That's boring as fuck. There are a couple documentaries out there on the pipeline of gay porn "talent". I watched one. You can reasonably extrapolate a lot of this stuff from it. I forget the name of it. I went through a phase of studying homosexuality from the homosexual's point of view in order to understand how they see themselves. It's no surprise that the proliferation of pornography coincides with the rise in homosexual political power.

The stewardess was right in this sweet spot of attention from men based on her appearance. With a good childhood, a woman holds herself out of that by covering up and marrying young. But most millennial and Zoomer girls have been raised totally defenseless against this kind of predation. This stewardess, probably unconsciously, reordered her appearance in order to match that of the typical pornstar. The Jenners and the Kardashians are instrumental in this. Through their appearances on grocery store magazine stands, tv commercials, shows, and tabloid websites, they constantly set a tone for "beauty" that the average, non-Nordic brunette can attain for themselves. None of them are all that good looking without their wiles. In fact, they're stumpy and godawful to look at. But they have shown the way for hundreds of millions of women. The rump and the pushup bra. The pushup bra predates them, of course, but they took it from a Western ideal of princesses and countesses to the down-home-hoe gutter where it wallows now. You know it's true. Kim's sex tape came out in 2007, filmed in 2003. Jamie Kennedy Experiment and Jackass were taking off about the time that sex tape was filmed. Personal degradation was already in-market at that point. Kim K. and Paris Hilton simply figured out how to sexualize it and ride the meteor into stardom. They were pioneers of Satanism. Let's hope they change!

This is the operating standard for most women nowadays. They're programmed. The fart girl next to me wishes she had the personal self-hatred of the stewardess. In her wine stupor, she'd settle for making out if the guy showed a romantic interest. In fact, that's probably what she'd like more than anything in the world: some schlub to watch the NFL with her. But the stewardess she worships in the same manner she worships Kim Kardashian (who's passing on the torch to the younger sister that also had an interracial baby). Stormi. What a stupid, demonic name. But it markets well. Extremely well. Damn it all to hell. Yes, this stewardess is a mini-goddess in our social matrix. She's the mechanical maw that chews up baby chicks in our poultry factories. She'll let the thug take her if he wanted. She was never Nordic anyway (in her mind) so why does it matter?

Death by orgasm. It happens in all manner of flavors to all manner of people.

Air travel should be banned, at least for thots. I don't want to live in the air the college girl farted in or the stewardess put lipstick on in. No doubt, some people on board were decent. I'd ride in a horse-drawn carriage next to them. But unless I have $5000 to fork out for a private flight, what's the worth in it? There's none for anyone but the very elite. And they want to kill everyone else because they see how much fun is spoiled when poor people are around. And what percentage of the West's current population would actually exist now and to what degree would there be a wealth disparity like there is now if Teddy hadn't run as Bull Moose and the 1890's immigration wave had never happened? We can only imagine. Look at those century old photos of Detroit. Look at how well everyone dressed. Do you really want to traverse in a tube full of Boomers, whores, and *others*? No, of course not. And of course, we can't outlaw airline travel because that would be a violation of the non-aggression principle and since we're supposed to, axiomatically, allow the "market to decide" – we should never impose our own personal bigotries onto others at the point of a gun. So, get rich or fuck off. But yeah, we should ban airline travel. What does it accomplish anyway? Only people who have cures to diseases or people who are charged with culling sub-85 IQ populations should be allowed to travel by air. What do I know? I'm not a dictator. This is all a joke.

Witch On-Stage

In 2007 or so, I was playing an open mic in Portland, OR. This strung-out early Gen-Xer took stage, doing his best Joe Walsh impression (hippy music). He was very polished, which was surprising cause he looked homeless. But the "soul" of his music was pure drug-abusing Oregon County Fair psychosis. His chord structures were strange. Everything was STRANGE. And it was clear he had been stewing in this weirdness for a very long time. Closed window shades and marijuana.

I joked to my guitarist friend about how someone should give this guy a $2 million recording contract. Set him up in one of those super studios in Santa Monica, put him with the best studio musicians, and just follow his weirdness wherever it went. I think *Walk Hard* characterized it a bit when the main character goes through his genius/Brian Wilson phase. But the character was depicted as having talent. This open mic dude did not have talent. Just a psychotic logic you could barely follow.

Make him Columbia Records' flagship rocker!!

Looking at Lily Singh's show, it reminds me of this joke I once made in 2007. She's been raised to distrust and dislike white people. She imbibed a hateful ideology of genocide. And now they're giving her the $2 million contract. She's psychotic and WEIRD. But there's a thin veneer of hip-hop and the trappings of a top-notch TV studio to make her palatable.

In a just society, she would be a homeless witch hunched over some drainage ditch - screaming to herself. She'd be in India, failed by her shitty parents and probably getting groomed to be a prostitute. Or she'd be in a call center, going home at night to slap the shit out of her kids and mother-in-law.

How long until they're doing sex change operations on-stage at the VMA's?

Help Me, I'm *Alienated*

"Modernity" is just government.

There's government everywhere now. The rich get that way off of selling out their own people, lands, and culture. Government allows them to do it. Corporations are just corny logs the government shits out.

John Adams, our second President, was so poor he had to live out of a rented room. He had no fagbag speaking tours, book deals, and Netflix money laundering to go on to. He had no children in Haiti to suck the adrenochrome out of.

All of this crazy shit is here because of 22 trillion in national debt, central banking, and 100+ trillion in unfunded liabilities, not to mention immigration amnesties and welfare for all. The corporations and large businesses in America have to reflect the resulting culture back to the people or they're not profitable, especially in the pre-Internet era.

Andrew Jackson was right to make war on the central bankers.

Maybe Trump will make war on them in his second term.

I think Boomer real estate developers are destroying America, riding off into the sunset drinking whiskey on their yachts (as Linkola put it).

But I also see how greedy, libfuck county commissioners raise property taxes YEAR AFTER YEAR, making horse grazing and hay cultivation completely unprofitable.

Cities in America are concentrations of psychosis. Roosh V is right to warn people to get out of them while there's still time. Everyone is grifting the fuck out of each other until it all blows up in race wars and other crazy, unpredictable shit.

It just so happens the worst cities are also run by DEMOCRATS! Haha, just kidding.

Clearly, white people are the only race with a penchant for Christianity and village societies. Even shitlibs who move to Bend, Oregon or Bozeman, Montana or Asheville, N.C. just try to lock down everything in time using government. Most white people like village looking societies.

It's just the fucks who build low income housing with property tax money that should be hung to death in the public square, in Minecraft the video game.

I tend to think that "the good guys" can wield government in order to peel back government.

I also sympathize with "breaking up the monopolies". The way I see of doing it isn't to seize domestic assets and put Bill Gates in a county jail for a week or something like this.

The way to do it is to renegotiate all these garbage trade deals, raise tariffs on competing nations, and quash immigration completely for 30 years.

Jeff Bezos is worth as much as he is directly because of NAFTA and China entering the WTO. All that shit you buy on Amazon comes from China. He gets to gawk around like a demi-god and alienate everyone because of dumbshit, corrupt grifters in Congress.

The wealthiest dudes I've ever known, who own golf courses in Nevada and shit like this, got their money by RUSHING to wherever government was intervening big time. Oil spill cleanups, hurricane disaster relief, changes in the financial laws, etc.

They all cut themselves in on deals like this.

There is SO MUCH money being made on illegal immigration. The Koch Brothers (well, I guess the one died so that's good) own the company that gets big government contracts for housing illegals. And they own the lobbying firm that convinces corrupt CIA grifters in Congress like Dan Crenshaw WHERE to funnel the money. The money's getting spent. It's a mad rush to determine WHERE.

Gymcel

"Go to the gym" becomes a cope, after a certain while, over the fact that whites are being dispossessed in their own homelands by the concentration of capital into finance (and away from the common man). The dispossession plays out in other ways, of course.

When you own more than an acre or two, suddenly you have plenty to keep you physically active. You get to raise animals, plant veggies, and entice women to make babies with you. You'll stay in shape and have all these stabilizer muscles in your back, shoulders, and hips working for you in a way that compound lifts and sprints don't. But all that is being ripped out of your callused, gym hands by corrupt "old people" who know the rules of democracy better than you do. And who raise your taxes so Somalia can be imported to your neighborhood.

Go to the gym as a nootropic so you can strategize on how to rip the power out of the hands of those old pieces of shit.

Lol, there's Pinochet doing pushups and taking ashwagandha pills he got off of the manosphere e-mail list.

It's unending curls and hemorrhaging your money away to grifters that makes you have that Dragon Energy physiognomy. NOT your plotting, scheming, strategizing, philosophizing, and power to convince others to pursue certain ends. That's just dorky gamma stuff.

Strategy Guide Moment #1

You're going to say to yourself, "Wow, Steve, you're saying this is a strategy guide for a video game but so much of what you describe fits reality perfectly."

To that, I say, "A) How do you know that I even wrote this book? -and- B) Who's to say art can't mimic reality or that the author of this book would draw from Steve Franssen's social media feed in establishing some of the strategy of this comedy video game world?"

You think this is a put on? You don't like your intellect being insulted? You don't see things clearly. You don't see that if this author didn't describe this video game, someone else would. Cop-out's could be had. We could turn to Simulation Theory and throw people off the scent that this video game isn't being made or that it is made by some unseen force that has yet to be described. That's dorky, though. Someone is making this video game. It's up to the gamers to sort it out. This book, termed a strategy guide, is a divination.

The Race

People without racial consciousness will tend toward the most certain of races "in the room". This is to say that they will gravitate toward the most ethnocentric race in the society. It is said that those who do not have a guiding philosophy in their life will gravitate toward the most certain person in the room. Well, this is also the case on a demographic scale.

Sam Francis asked if Western Civilization could be carried on without the white race. It cannot. And so, in the early years of mass migration, the highest caliber of Third Worlders came to the West to be absorbed into the white race. But there's not enough white to go around and now Western Civilization is atrophying. There must be a 30-40 year immigration moratorium so that any intermarriage that carries on will not erode the capacity for those who remain ethnocentrically European to not be swamped out and a techno-Communist Babel to emerge from the overarching domination of the highly ethnocentric Jewish and Asian races.

Are these statements racist as fuck? Nah. This is simply the truth and you're not allowed to say it. But I am past the point of caring. I am not angry. I am not full of hatred. I love the true genetic diversity of distinct peoples who are proud of who they are. I'm like a happy zoologist. You can be the happiest zoologist when it comes to mammals, insects, birds, etc. You get cozy zoo gigs, have TV shows come interview you, and go on all the late-night talk shows where everyone fawns over your handling skills of the various species in the domain. Do this at an intellectual level with humans and suddenly you're the target of all manner of hatred. I say ENOUGH! Grow up! Time for us to get honest about how people are different. It's not something to be afraid of. It won't lead to mass genocide. It won't lead to fascist uprisings. In fact, the suppression of these facts is precisely what will lead to those happenings. Being a happy zoologist doesn't make you *hate* a race different than yours. If you can reasonably expect to be embargoed for speaking the truth about race, how long can you resist becoming radicalized? How long must happy zoologists endure their own evisceration for having simple observations? So long as the corporate media and intelligence agencies, foreign and domestic, have their say – it will be another while yet.

Time Vampires

Time vampires want to give the illusion of giving value while putting the fangs to you on one of your blind spots. Time vampires probe and probe. They watch from a distance and then pounce, announcing they're engaging you in good faith as they emotionally drain you. They do not speak openly. They are not spiritually Christian. They do not have Christian consciousness. They have become malignant atheists who believe that because there is no physical evidence of the Spirit, the Spirit cannot be indicative of some profound process going on at a genetic level within the inheritors of Christ. They exist in a void. They are dying. And your blood is poison to them. It is not sustenance. That is a great misnomer. They embrace the void. They want more emptiness. In their inverted world, your blood is a curse. They live off the curse. You, of course, experience the inverse. You experience the loss of vitality as something evil. They simply experience void. The opposite of good isn't evil. It is nothingness.

You ward away time vampires by hacking and slashing like a Teutonic knight anytime anyone crosses that red line on the ground. You must be ruthless and unconquerable. You must push the Saracen back across the border. There is no doubt. Doubt only delays you. It only gives the vampire a foothold. This is an easy equation. There is no complexity to it. Anyone who convinces you of complexity is paralyzing you so that other time vampires can come in and do the same.

Our heritage is that of paying for someone's time. We gather and chop wood. We fish from the ocean. We unite under God. We weave. We dance and sing. We story tell. But we never draw others into the void. We do not induce boredom as a habit. That tendency has been programmed into us by an alien media and schooling system. Our schooling system once *was* Prussian. Now it is openly Satanic. Never forget that the composition of a society dictates its institutions. We have forgotten who we are precisely because there is so much that is alien in our midst.

Never allow another man to massage your expectations of him with flattery. That is not our way. For centuries, for millennia, we greeted by shaking hands and looking one another in the eyes. This is the measure of a man. And those who make a big show of this by shaking too hard or towering-over like a Lyndon Johnson have learned the tools of manipulation of the time vampires. These false barbarians are estranged from their own race.

Time vampires love the art of flattery. They love the art of professing respect. They always go above and beyond in the deceptive arts. They never employ simple deceptions. A simple deception is all that has ever been needed in our common law. I will not name these simple deceptions because I refuse to arm the outgroup. The eyes of the world are watching. This is my simple deception. Go a step further and you will discover the truth.

Act like a man. Smash the time vampire. Stab him in the heart with a stake. It's easy. Remember the psychological context within which the vampire arose to prominence in our Western lore. Go a step further here.

We've Noticed You're Using An Adblocker

Oh, you have, have you? Maybe I should stop checking your website. In fact, this 'halt' and raise of the hand you've put before me is enough to disinterest me entirely from your enterprise, faggot. Your information source has never been enough to inspire and encourage me. I have only ever checked it to know 'what is going on' but in truth, you don't know what's going on. You're a fucking retard with more money than me. That's all it boils down to.

When I give you my attention, you eventually extract more money from me. I can't, in good conscience, keep up this ugly dance. I can't allow you to speak to me this way. I can't help you make the corporate payola you feel entitled to. Thank you, actually. Thank you for noticing I'm using an Adblocker. You can't "adblock" in the real world. You get sent to prison immediately. Thank you for reminding me that I hate how you are polluting the world and subduing my people with state goons and billboards. You have arranged it so that you are untouchable. My adblock is my reminder that I have human dignity. Perhaps you were even decent at one point. But now the game is clear. Now you show me you are allied with the child rapists.

Screed

A man walks up to me and says, "This book is mean, rude, angry, and critical. How dare you!"

Then I say, "Perhaps it is all those things. I'll tell you what it isn't: cynical." This person will visit from time to time, hooked on that *cynical* word. He or she will have philosophical justifications.

The person responds, "You are not allowed to say these things out loud. I will ruin your life if you go even one step further."

I have given up caring. I will say what is on my mind. If I look like a madman, I don't care. If people feel threatened, remember, these are words. Should someone decide to put me under suspicion, I don't care. I am helping so many people now. I am serving the right cause. I am aligning with the best ones out there. We are going to rebuild the world. There is nothing you can do to stop us. This may be a screed but at least it's real. I make no apologies.

My Poor Boys

You can name them. But do it in a way they can't characterize. You either go full force or you do it subtly, at a level they have to work to reach. They with all their spare time. The proclivity is everywhere. Theirs is a disease. And they hold the power of life and death. We're working to change that. Then everyone can, more or less, get back to the way it was. Only, we will be consciously armed against their dialectic. Personally, I have more fun doing it in a way they can't characterize. I have read their texts. I know their spiritual orientation. I have gotten as close to believing without believing as possible. No, I will never bear their mark on me. Even if they force it on my body, my conscience will be clean. These are not the ones you think I'm suggesting, at least if you're unpolished and new to my works. Think beyond that. Notice the arrangements being made. The ones you think I'm talking about you can't go full force on. No, I'm talking about my poor boys. You know now. Don't get distracted. They're everywhere. They're your poor boys, too. Remember. Remember how they dropped like flies. It's a sickness.

Ayn Rand Did More Harm Than Good

Fuck that bitch. She pretended there wasn't mystery. You stupid bitch. You fucking cunt. It's time to redeem her victims. Highest-selling philosophical book of all time and the actual content was rape and industrialist idolatry. Voted most influential! Ayn Rand was a cunt and I would say it to her face. You joyless witch. You psychological leftover of Communism. Fucking useless. Completely psyoped a whole generation of intellectuals on what made the West great.

Should have deported her for being poor when we had the chance.

People who have taken her seriously have gone on to ruin our people and done it in a way they haven't had to have compunctions about. The worst autists, the Landmark Forum, Tony Robbins, the libertarians, the OBJECTIVISTS are time vampires. They are uninspired retards. And they'll suck out your time with their awkward certainty. They'll go to a nice restaurant with you and act like heads on a swivel. All they can do is act like heads on a swivel. They've lost their humanity. BUT they know that if they form a psychological and intellectual matrix thick enough, you will lose your own humanity in the subsequent search. Nathaniel Branden *helped* that stupid bitch. He put his cock in her. He rebelled, so that's something. He kept a wee bit more of his humanity. He didn't stab the West in the heart like she did. She should have stabbed herself in the heart and bled. Instead she smoked and smoked. Anxious bitch. Learn to play the lute, you dumb bitch. Go for a walk on the Irish coast, you money whore. Fuck money whores. They live in hell. They bitch and moan and complain when they don't get enough. She lived in a cancer cell. She was a cancer cell. She was dumb. She pretended with her piercing eyes and her stimulants but actually, she was dumb. Not smart. Assertive, for a woman, sure. Dumb!

If I saw Ayn Rand today, I wouldn't break the non-aggression principle. Are you kidding me? I wouldn't spit on her! I wouldn't bulldog her at her own game. I would just stare at her. I would win the staring contest. I am smarter. I don't have to pretend. She would shrivel like a time vampire. And all her little suckling faggot followers would shrivel with her. Oh no, Mama was bested by Papa! Oh no, Papa is dominating Mama! Oh no, Papa won't take Mama's shit anymore. That's right, you dumb bitch. You stupid bitch. I am the king. Oh, you don't like that? Too bad, I already beat your arguments. All I had to do was stare at you.

Some other madman who wasn't me would slap the cigarette out of her wiry mouth. Probably graze her face and make her stumble back like the fat witch from Hansel and Gretel. But not me. I have the stare. I have the argument. I win.

Strategy Guide Moment #2 (Hit Pause!)

Making fun of Ayn Rand in reality would be a most abhorrent and patently false amalgamation of verbal abuse. She stood against the mob! Never has a mob ever achieved anything but violence and mayhem. It's in the definition of the word. (Jorden Peterson voice) The West is polarized, you see? I never would have imagined that long-haul truckers and people that, you know, work repetitive tasks for long periods of time would ever gravitate toward my work. But I was wrong!

I Didn't Choose The Tool

Don't blame me. Don't rope me into your cynicism. I didn't make the damn thing. The damn thing is in my way. It's in everyone's ways. That's the point. You can't go anywhere without dealing with it in some way. You are not *beyond*. We are all bound. Don't be a fool. Stop running away. We can't persist without it because everyone just gets in the way if you try. We have to outgrow it. I dare say collectively. How many of us will it take? I don't know. I don't think it's *everyone*. They're just inventing the wheel over there. Let's not be foolish, either.

It's simply not up to me to choose the saturation point. Nor is it up to you and no, you haven't dawned upon the answer before everyone else. Otherwise, your way would have seen a breakout already – as you are already living it. Nobody is living *it*. We're not there yet. But I think everyone is eager to get there. That's obvious. Some aren't, though. Oops. They're either stupid like animals or they want to wallow in it because deep down they feel empty. I know you feel something. I feel a lot of it. All the time. I'm eager to get past this point but it can't be rushed and you can't fake it. We have to walk *through*. It will take some time. No shortcuts. Shortcuts lead to Hell. Every time. Let's do it the right way.

I didn't choose this. Don't blame it on me. When the time comes, we'll leave together.

Ayn Rand Was Ugly

I'm not here to rail against free markets. Obviously, governments and idiot "businessmen" petition government to fuck over their competitors, import serf classes from Aztlán, and depress wages while concentrating capital into finance. These fuckwits get away with it because nobody is willing to physically prevent them. Beyond that, they have the public so gaslit that anyone who dares oppose them is "LARPing". It's depressing to realize how many of our top-flight intellectuals can't piece together this basic equation. In fact, they embody the "make fun of LARPers" mindset they've been abused with for generations.

There's nothing wrong with standing "against the mob" until you realize the emotional, psychological, spiritual, and philosophical bankruptcy of doing it for the wrong reasons. I'm a brave atheist standing up against Christians! Shut the fuck up. I'm a brave capitalist standing against the meddling regulators while international bankers operate in the background! Shut the fuck up. I smoke cigarettes, remain childless, and pay no lip service to the importance of transmitting wealth intergenerationally! Shut the fuck up, lady. Close your legs, for God's sakes. Oh wait, God doesn't exist because there's no proof and the charlatans who manipulate the masses using philosophy always place God just beyond the realm of human knowledge. Shut the fuck up. We're dying out here and you're doing your best John Galt impression. That's what Ayn Rand did. She was a titanic baby, abused stimulants, idealized autistic rape, and expected the rest of society to take care of her because she paid lip service to capitalism. Fuck you, you cosmopolitan cunt. Talk about paving the way for subsequent generations of high-brow intellectuals eager to fuck Yeoman America out of its last remaining goodness. Hey, strip miners are mixing their labor with the land! Who are you to object? You're not a *statist*, are you?

Obviously, consuming energy at ever-increasing rates is universally preferable. Ayn Rand showed us as much by the bravery of her cigarette abuse. While small-brained, moblike journalists flashed their crucifixes at her – she dazzled us all by puffing on her death stick with the glare of a thousand suns. We should suck all the life out of those thousand suns! Especially the Chinese and the Indians should do it. Why are we more deserving than the Chinese and the Indians? We aren't! We're all just humans. Let the market decide. You really think you've got it more figured out than the markets? Statist! Trust the genius of the markets. There's enough for all of us. You should never say mean things about other nations raping the environment to death. If we're really nice always and forever, that will convince sub 85 IQ nations to embrace the principles of the free market. Then we can all team up, put pipelines down into the Earth's core, and then terraform Mars. That's the way it works! By sucking the life out of the planet, we actually resolve the problem of global *underpopulation*. The Chinese and the Indians are ready to team up with us. We should never ever be mean to them. What do I care if my Chinese neighbor roasts live dogs to death over open pits in his backyard on the other side of my wooden fence? So long as there's *no government*, I don't care. I would just say that what he was doing was aesthetically negative, that eventually it would weigh heavy on his conscience and he would lose self-esteem, and I would sell my rapidly depreciating house so I could move to be with more white people in a covenant community. What do I care that whole swaths of the Intermountain West are being colonized by Mexicans and picture-taking Chinese?

Once we have no government, we'll all just be friendly neighbors. No, I won't vote to change this trend. That just makes me a participant in government. 100% of all things government does is wrong because taxation is theft. So no, I'm only going to support my preferred Presidential candidate implicitly by defending his free speech, not by engaging in political activism or by crushing his enemies by any peaceable means possible. The truth will eventually come out and then all races of the world above a 115 IQ will embrace the truth of free markets and Ayn Rand's legacy will be intact even though she never accounted for race and actually distracted whites from racial consciousness on a large-scale right when they needed racial consciousness the most.

She wasn't a double agent. She was just a confused woman with a bad childhood. She had a bad childhood, you know. She almost came from a single mother household but actually she came from a no-parent household. Everything she did was by her own bootstraps, just like me. Ayn Rand

and I did things the same way. And we are both champions of the free market. She's like a mother to me, even though she didn't have a maternal bone in her body. That's okay by me. The women in my life *love* rational debate. Ayn Rand helped them to be that way. But you have to leave out the bad when you consider different philosophers. Like the cigarette smoking. That's bad. That's coping with childhood trauma. But the rapacious, wanton greed that forms the crusty intellectualized shield over the sucking wound of childhood trauma? That's cool. Take 90 minutes of your life to watch a video of me and a Jew discussing how fucking cool it is to suck the life out of the planet, just so long as no *governments* are doing it. I'm not spiritually dead because remember, there's never been any verifiable evidence that the body contains a spirit. That movie *21 Grams* is bullshit and I have done the scientific research to show that that one guy rigged the scales. Anyway, it can't be replicated – so fuck the notion of the existence of a "spirit". Fuck any curiosity anyone could ever have that it is a profound metaphor for some kind of racial consciousness inherent to a certain people. Or that a lack of evidence doesn't actively negate a hypothesis. No, be a Non-Spiritual Outsider like me. Like Ayn Rand. We know The Way. After all, our metaphysics check out. You may feel uncomfortable around us but because you can't articulate it in any clear terms, clearly you are self-attacking because my philosophy is hurting your False Self. Any resistance against this idea is an insult to my tremendous prestige, pedigree, training, and intellectual heritage.

Ayn Rand was a cunt. I'd say it to her face. But that's not philosophical. That's verbal abuse! This is wrong. Who will have the courage to stop me in my dastardly deed?! She was the finest philosopher of the 20th century. It wasn't somebody else. Hong Kong is the way that it is because of Christianity and capitalism. It doesn't matter that an Anglo elite pursued their ethnic self-interests by establishing Hong Kong as a trading colony. It doesn't matter that the Cantonese they partnered with and mentored are being swept aside by a rising tide of Han Chinese. This is Capitalism vs. Socialism: The Final Showdown. Ayn Rand would have loved this. I bear testament to her by eating this Indian buffet right here in the heart of Kowloon. She would be so happy with me. These brave Hong Kongese souls are motivated by *freedom.* Remember, it was extremely important to them *before* they were under duress by a Chinese government that wants to harvest dissidents for their organs. The Hong Kongese are not making appeals to America because of its history of an interventionist foreign policy. They are seeking to connect with our brave contingent of ancaps who KNOW the arguments Ayn Rand and Murray Rothbard put forth. They are not motivated by the fear of being put in camps and having psychotic surgeries done on them. They know squarely that it is Christianity and Capitalism that makes their society work. Those ethnic Han in their midst, waving red flags and getting in street brawls, are simply not aware of the Randian metaphysics. Their IQ's are high enough. They can "get it"! After all, the Cantonese "get it". They're definitely going to hold on to what they learned from the English, for centuries to come. Even if they go the way of Tibet (who cares about them at this point anyway?), it's clear that they will always be minarchists. But it's because they *learned* minarchism. It's not because they're some Asian bizarro sub-strain. It's because Ayn Rand cigarettes.

This defiance is 100% because of childhood trauma. It's not defiance. It's sarcasm! Even though the author wasn't treated with sarcasm until middle school and he already exhumed the feelings of humiliation battered into him by fuckwit public school teachers, sarcasm is intrinsically bad and it is never actually defiance! It's at someone else's expense and actually in a stateless society there would never be competition, just self-interested parties cooperating and having a spirited "to-and-fro". There's no fight in the dog. It is programmed into him in middle school. He is just hard-up for validation from authority figures, who he projects sarcasm onto. It's not because he already figured out the need for validation from authority figures, took care of it by getting more plugged into *his* life, and had the courage to speak out against the abuses of his tormentors in a way that would totally disarm them. He is not accurately reflecting back to these false authority figures their own contempt. He is not a tuning fork. He is not an antenna tower. He is arrogant! He is sarcastic! He is a toxic abuser who should be ostracized and gaslit for being "sadistic". It's not the false certainty of his authority figures that is sadistic. It's not their complete lack of receptivity to accurate feedback that is sadistic. No, he has a bad attitude and should be indicted for calling Ayn Rand a cunt. No person who has healed a great deal of their childhood trauma would ever dare call Ayn Rand a cunt. That's simply impossible. Fuck the dog. Rape the planet. Oh, that's myopic, leftie talk. Don't look up the Irish elk. Don't look up big game hunting records from the 1800's, when our government was 5% the size it is today. Don't notice how the size of moose was rapidly dwindling even then. There are no variations of anarcho-capitalism. There is only the genius of the market. Ayn Rand came up with that. We're going to use moose meat to power Chinese Tesla rockets to Mars so we can fuck the everloving shit out of the subterranean Martians and use their meat and tech to power our expansion to one of Saturn's moons. Get in the way of that and you're Antifa, the real fascists. Geniuses are never insomniacs because of the effort it takes to pick through the shitshow that previous geniuses left in their wakes. They're sleepless because they have *trauma*. Duh!

Late Night Dodgeball

NON-STOP CANNED LAUGHTER

JJ: *Hi there. I'm Jimmy James. Call me JJ! I'm the host of Later Night Show. I'm fucking gay! Today I'm in an SUV and seated next to...*

MO: Grahhh! This is Michelle Obama. This little cracker bitch seated next to me is corny. Haha! Beyoncé, what what?

Imma beat his bitchass in volleyball just to prove a bitch ain't shit. Whatchu gunna do, you little faggot? America!

JJ: Haha! This is funny. Yes, I'll be representing Team England. It's an all-male team. We all have remote dildos in our butts. When we hit a woman from the all-female Team America, the vibrators go off in our butts. This is the way the Beatles would have wanted things.

MO: Ladies, assemble. On mah team is Beyoncé, the fat white bitch from SNL, and Mexican Tampon. We gonna use blue balls, haha! Ya heard? We gonna hit these whitebois with blue balls. Yam yam.

JJ: I'm a little queer male. Yes, Team America is going to win. That's for certain. My gay team has the men who take it in the butt the most. I have the little manboy from Spiderman. Also joining us is Benedict Cumballs. And lastly we have Harry, the British Subject. He is Indian and gay. He has tattoo sleeves.

Fat SNL Bitch: Omg! I am eating sandwiches. I am so fat and stupid. Middle America women are fucking stupid and corny. I'm kind of a man. I play police in movies and I kick men in the balls. I'm going to eat myself to death and I fucking hate you. Ready for Team America!

Indian Harry: *I don't feel comfortable playing for Team England because I have an American accent and I am a rootless transnational brought over on a work visa. I am ready for pussy. All I eat is pussy. And I can rap and use a loop machine. Rapping and pussy. Rapping the pussy.*

JJ: *You cis-gendered fuckwit! You're supposed to act more British. You're on Team England. Act like it, at once or I will reveal my penis to you backstage.*

Indian Harry: *Hello, guvna! Blimey, Harry Potter!*

CANNED LAUGHTER THROUGHOUT

Mexican Tampon: Where is the net? Like, the white man is going to catch us? I am strange. I am acting weird. This is funny. I bring a taco with me. I am drinking cerveza. There is many makeup on my face.

JJ (to Benedict Cumballs): *Oy, Benny! My body is soft and supple from all the anal action backstage. Look how my pelvis slouches, withered and beaten by my producers. I will wiggle my bug arms at you and chant a British chant and you will smile because you are a bigtime movie star. You know the game but you have to pretend to be attracted to women. That is the difference between us, you and me! (Benedict pretends to be awkward).*

MO: Yo, I been trained by the best producers and acting coaches to be a fucking bitch and y'all white bitches ain't shit, amirite? Imma shake my hands at you and be real loud. Mexican Tampon gets me, dontcha sista? We gon' get it like in 2008. Black people are superior to corny white folks!

Team America sings Beyonce song

Team England is awkward and gay

Referee: Are you ready, Team America? Are you ready, Team England? Okay, race war!

Announcer: Benedict throws and misses. He throws like a bitch! Fat SNL Bitch immediately throws and gets him out. Now Michelle Obama is getting really angry and she throws. She gets JJ out by hitting him in the balls. He is wiggling his hips as he goes back to the bench. Indian Man is hit right in the balls by Mexican Tampon. And now Spiderman is all by himself on Team England. Michelle Obama hits him right in the balls – OOH! That's going to leave a mark. That was the nutshot heard round the world with Team USA going up 1 to 0. His balls must be hurting so much!

Team USA are punching their fists in the air and acting like men! This is the natural order. This is the way of things. They are going to kick the shit out of Team England. Let's go have a look at Team England as they reel from their stunning loss at the hands of the strong, proud women.

Oh, hahaha! They're drinking tea. Classical music is playing. These boneheads are touching each other effeminately and Cumballs is reloading the batteries on the dildos. Weird white men. We hate white men, especially in America!

Game Two, here we go! Team USA is on those balls like a bunch of whores that are amazing, independent women. And Team England gets one of them out. Mexican Tampon gets NAILED right in the boobs. Her silicon bags burst. This is getting ugly, folks! The Indian Man is tagged out and is hit again as he goes down. Now he is flailing and it's really funny, like Funniest Home Videos. The rest of Team USA is tagged out because they're incompetent and useless, setting up a final round.

Brief Cutaway Scene

Benedict Cumballs: *Here you go, Mrs. Obama. This is your shitty book and I want to nurse at your titty. May I please have the honor of your signature? Yes, thank you. I am in love with the Obamas.*

CANNED LAUGHTER, SCENE CUTS BACK TO FINAL MATCH

Announcer: And we're off! Team USA operating now with the advantage of fully auto AK-47's. They are simply SLAUGHTERING Team England at this point! There it is, Team England loses immediately and who could have expected anything else. There is carnage everywhere. Lesbians are more powerful than homosexual men. Michelle Obama is waving bye-bye and the SNL Bitch is porking down another sandwich. Feminism is hilarious! That's it for us tonight on the Later Night Show. We hope you kill yourselves but remember, do it responsibly and slowly. Goodnight, folks!

Women Have Less Free Will Than Men

My friend, I am so sorry you have walked down this dark path of ideology. My deepest sympathies on your mother having less free will than your father. There is no chance in heck that things were that way because that's the natural order. I'm even uncomfortable using that phrase, "natural order". Since there are no deep analytical statistics that reveal to us the *exact* degree to which women have less free will than men, it is easy to infer that women have just as much free will as men. You are simply wrong in your assertation and that is, my friend, not an argument. You are simply trying to estrange women from men when you assert that they have less free will than men. You are not trying to bring order to our society. You are sowing the seeds of (dramatic pause for effect) chaos!

Your mother failed to demonstrate to you a woman with free will. My deepest sympathies. And that her mother and her grandmother also failed to actualize their free will is simply the riddle of intergenerational trauma unveiling itself. But of course, peaceful parenting is the absolute solution. The women in my life have full free will and would never ever follow some kind of strong man into a patriarchal order. That is wrong. I can't believe that you can't see it's wrong. My gosh! I am aghast! The women in my life, who have full free will, would use rational debate to stem back the tide of a strongman revolution. I did *not* train them to my preferences. They simply auto-generated a love for rational debate and analysis. That's what women do! They have debates with one another and analyze things in the absolute profoundest of terms. I love the women in my life. I spend all of my time with them. They are just as philosophical as men. The strains of childbearing and rearing are insufficient to inhibit in them a more analytical manner of being. Their naturally-occurring total free will manifests itself in wanting to have children young in life but then absolutely wanting careers in the second half of life, no matter what. They don't have to be cajoled, manipulated, subtly influenced, steered, or had their trauma worked on actively by me, someone who is a master of philosophy but cannot claim any formal training in psychology.

Women strike out, bold and courageous, in unabashed examinations of truth. They post on Twitter about the philosophical meals they cooked. They scratch at socialist heads of state with philosophical claws. They definitely never disengage from the culture war once they've found a strong man who will carry the awful, personality distorting weight they've been carrying by using their inborne gifts for seduction and persuasion in order to prevent themselves from being raped by Tyrone.

Yes, women have full free will. You are mistaken, my friend. Don't scrutinize my personal decisions. There is no truth to be learned there. Women are profound thinkers and tacticians. You have become cynical and it's because your mother provoked cynicism in you. Her free will was eroded by feminism. She actually would have had free will completely and totally if it weren't for *propaganda*. Never mind that women who are exposed to better philosophies, the traditional sort that have served mankind for eons, seem to bend to the will of strong men who prefer order. See, the woman is doing that because of free choice and not out of some kind of survival instinct that kicks in when Tyrone has managed to break down the door, so to speak. She will gladly subsume the entirety of herself into another tribe in order so that she won't be raped to death and that's the way it has always been. She does that out of free will. A strong woman with her full free will is the dividing line between a world of chaos and destruction and a world of order and beauty. See, women and men are equal – in a sense. We must listen to women, especially when they bring their free will to bear on matters of business, war, and philosophy. Once they have the flower of self-knowledge, there is nothing intrinsic to them that leaves them susceptible to the most certain social force in the environment. Then they simply love rational debate and analysis.

Ayn Rand, Get Some

Dear Ayn,

You suck. Your entire adulthood was an amphetamine-fueled, intellectualized tantrum for attention. You characterized collectives as evil in nature and that the West has been a history of the individual against the collective. But you failed to interpret what made the West so wonderful: our collectives were largely voluntary, race-based, and every man was a sheriff. Sometimes a great individual emerged from this milieu but always and forever the quality of the collective was inexorably tied to the quality of the individual. The average IQ of Florence supported the greatness of the Medicis. Anyway, good try, you bitch. I'm glad you lived so we could get "greed is good" memed into us. And so intellectuals could have more implements by which to convince us that there is no such thing as greed.

Terrorist Farms

Being deep in the "ancap scene" a number of years back, and all the disregard and paralysis of racial consciousness it begets, a person close to me came to know a former "moderate" Muslim born and raised in the upper Midwest.

This "moderate" Muslim, who's a Millennial, disclosed that in the mosques they teach the kids to hate America, hate whites, and feel contempt for the Founding. They do this only in Arabic and only when the room has been swept for recording devices.

I have been told similar stories about other "religions" in America.

Really gets the old noggin' joggin'. You start to realize that every religion inevitably has political expression.

Church and state are not separated and can never be. Every religion has a moral code. Moral code is always codified into law. Western common law is largely a reflection of pre-schism Christianity. I'm sure some nerdy pagan would pounce on me at this point. Fine, we'll allot something in there for pagans so they feel satisfied. Just kidding. The Catholic Church had a massive hand in setting the Western world in order. So did the Protestant movement into the United States. We had a Jeffersonian order not because of abstract philosophical principles but because of the "operating system" passed down through the generations and especially codified into a uniquely predisposed population, a sub-species if you will.

The Pursuit of Beauty

America is going through some "growing pains" right now. There's a little town near where I live. Little, compared to most of the rest of America, but too busy and noisy for me. I get gasoline there. Some contractors have just finished putting in some townhouses with 3,000 sq. ft. lots. Fiber cement siding in sand tan. The cheap, non-architectural roof shingles. Cheapest lighting fixtures. Concrete pads for parking put in directly outside the houses but no concrete or asphalt lane poured in for the little inlets that go to the townhomes. Probably 40 townhomes packed into 2 square acres. It's horrifying.

Now, I am not disparaging the poor. I'm not all that well-off myself. It wasn't so long ago that I had a considerable debt in my name and was renting too small of an apartment for my needs. I respect the struggle. I respect "the grind" (terrible way to characterize it). I'll take a buttfuckton of shoddy Montana craftsman style townhomes packed into too small a space over those Soviet stack-and-packs littered everywhere in Miami, Minneapolis, and other liberal shitholes. Still, the townhouses are hideous. And the people who live in them are transient. They have no economic permanence because mass migration has disenfranchised them.

To me, it's horrifying what's happening in Montana. They're carving up the countryside with 1400 sq. ft. houses called "ranchettes". Basically, all the Boomers made out like bandits and now they're having retirement homes built for them away from the creeping tide of the third world invasion of America. They buy too many horses and run them over their tiny lawns. I can't say I blame them for wanting to get away. Of course, I blame them for having a heavy hand in creating these circumstances. What so many attribute to "unfettered capitalism", I attribute to "unfettered state growth". Consumer credit appeared and everyone forgot their yeoman roots in the madhouse greed stampede that ensued. The welfare state appeared and everyone decided to fuck each other instead of talking out their problems in group settings. I understand.

It's still horrifying. I go to the local GOP rally and talk to a lady. Hi hunny, she says. I'm from Texas. Oh, I say. I ask her how big her lot is. She says, I dunno, darlin'. Maybe 1 acre? Oh yeah, lady? When did you move here? Well, we retired a couple years ago and thought we'd come live here. We moved in as soon as our house was built.

This is a Trump voter. Nice lady. Kind to me. But she is just looking for somewhere whiter, like her childhood, where she can watch TV until she dies. Did I mention people like her use the medical services here if they have a stomachache? It's covered!

Her existence is ugly. Was it shaped by forces beyond her control? I think so, at least to a degree. You can't attack people for their ignorance, can you? I'm not sure.

The real estate agents in Montana strut around like they're hot shit. They're selling off a land they never settled, always into smaller parcels. Their politics are fucking dogshit and there's no consequences for them. See them on the billboards? They're hot shit! Professionals! They have a "group". Do you know Sotheby's? Have you heard of the prestigious Berkshire Hathaway? It's all very fancy. It's a *feeding frenzy* when a new subdivision goes in and the developer hasn't partnered with a realty agency yet. Money! Am I being a bad ancap by opposing this? Am I being a leftist ideologue consumed by envy for thinking this stinks? No. And a big "frack you" to people who would imply so. I won't be silenced. There's a swindle going on. And it's getting so far out of control that Montana is no longer "the last best place". It's becoming a fucking strip mall, just like the rest of America. Oh, you like *A River Runs Through It*? Sorry pal, we need apartment buildings so the Mexicans can finally come here.

Oh, you like cowboys and Wyoming? Too bad! Evanston is filled with Chinese, there's a Muslim community in Gillette, and the university in Laramie is bringing many stellar athletes to our community!

Oh, you like Idaho because it's "quiet"? Wait till you see how many apartment buildings the HUSTLER Mormons are building in Idaho Falls and Pocatello. Oops, some of those buildings have refugees in them. Oops! Coeur D'Alene is pretty? Time for a fuckton of California hipsters to move there so their Instagram profiles can provoke envy in their wage-earning Netflix watching, wine-drinking, mushroom dabbling friends back home.

There's a creeping hideousness. People living in formerly beautiful, wholesome places have no recourse because posting a sign outside your house or business that says "No Democrats" (wink, wink) is not allowed. You can't say "No Genital Butcherers" outside your kitschy tapas restaurant and so...Bozeman, Montana has white people! Just go there and open a tapas restaurant.

Okay, we've waded through the shit. We did it so we can pursue beauty. How are we going to reinstitute freedom of association, which is more fundamental than freedom of

it is, because our electorate continues to squander the wealth of generations past. The old growth trees are gone and while the population should be meandering down a bit like the Japanese, instead it continues to explode because lobbyists can't get enough help around the house.

The children are sometimes beautiful. Some of them, quite frankly, have too much of their parents' shit loaded into them already. Some of them are alien. But some of them are beautiful. Children are beautiful, right? I like the Zoomers. They're forming an army.

There's beauty. I know a lot of it. Sometimes I let it slip but I hate casting pearls before swine. Why should we make it widely known? Why should I like a person who posts certain places to their Instagram? Shouldn't they be silenced? Who is going to make them stop? Will the marketplace of ideas eventually catch up to them and they'll quiet themselves? Maybe. Hopefully this book helps in that direction. Does it hurt that until then, maybe I will sometimes feel tempted to tell them to shut the fuck up and stop mining what's left? Yes. Parents do this all the time with their kids. They mine their kids for social media points. Stop fucking do that. Your children aren't a Twitter banner. Start conserving what's been handed to you. Start dissuading people from ruining all the beauty. Start treating people who deliberately make hideousness in the world the way they deserve to be treated: with scorn and an assertion of what is beautiful. The world is full of bad taste. The world is full of government, intermixing, and wanton ruin. Push back. I won't give away the beauty like a sellout. You'll have to fucking pry it out of me.

The Expensive Books

Light a cigar. Let's get a bit of that piano going. A calm touch of Gershwin. It's got to be ordered. No jazz. None of that jazz shit. But a foreigner would think it was jazz. The lights are lowered. You in your tweed suit. Me in my smoking jacket. Deep brown leather chairs. Nice rugs on the floor. It took my father 20 years to put this place together and I've been working on it for 10.

We're going to crack open the expensive books. See this one? Cost me $200 at the time. That's $250 in today's dollars. This one cost me $75. Got it cheap. The binding's not too bad, either.

Of course, you have your expensive books, too. We've read most of them. It's a nice life of leisure here. The bookcases I keep mine in are not quite as nice as yours but I pride myself on the depth of my selection. Yours is a bit less distinguished but that's why we're at my place today and not yours.

This is a lovely feeling. I would like to share it with people like me. Not all of them feel this way. Some of them are programmed against us. They would destroy this. They don't have the time. That's what it boils down to, doesn't it?

We're running out of time. It's getting choked off from us. I don't like that. I like the time it takes to understand this book here. It cost me $1000, believe it or not. They only did one printing and it's been out of print for 80 years. There's a reason it was forced out of print. You didn't know? You didn't catch the drift on that one? Yes, they forced him out. He was spitting mad at the time. He found another publisher but it was never the same for him after that.

If they could come by the window and peer in, they would preach to us about minimalism. It's minimalism that extends the time, you see! That's just austerity stripped of its spiritual roots. A nasty racket they have going for themselves. We'll keep them out as long as possible. These books are calling to us. Yes, good to keep company with you, old boy. That's passé, isn't it? Should I call you "Groyper"?

Millennials Off-Grid

Off-grid channels on YouTube sometimes catch my eye. I see these younger, 20 or 30-something couples busting their butts to make some place in the woods work for them. I'm not so into the tiny house thing. It's okay. I like the ones who are doing it for personal, philosophical reasons. I don't know if I would do what they're doing. Maybe. Should probably attempt it while I'm younger.

I like the idea of doing a Kirsten Dirksen style YouTube channel where I go around interviewing white people who fucked off to the woods because they can't stand the living-shithole America has become. Rather than this Zen focus on how their spaces are livable, I would ask them which races and cultures they don't like. Of course, a lot of people are doing it because government's way too big in the cities. But some of them are doing it because they genuinely don't enjoy living in close proximity with other peoples. I don't fault them. I just like the honesty angle of it. The channel wouldn't be funny. It would be sad, more than anything. At least it would be honest. You're not allowed even a shred of freedom of association. Corporations can shred your balls for being a conservative but heaven forbid a small business owner keep out a gangbanger or some sassy Filipina who smacks her lips too loudly as she's yacking on the phone in *a different language.* I understand why people are taking to the hills. Thank goodness for the electoral college. Once Texas turns blue, it's all fucked. Yes! I know! I am pushing back against it. But let's not be naïve douchebags and make *zero* considerations or preparations for what is a near statistical certainty at this point. Anyone who depicts such backup efforts as "accelerationism" or "collapse-idealizing" are fuckwads who should be barred from commerce. I can't stand people who infect others with their own self-doubt. Just because you have decided to take an ideological posture by pretending to be the Good Guy so hard that you don't help others, in fact try to put shame into them for thinking some bad shit is going to happen, doesn't mean that I need to put up with you or that you get to continue fucking people over while considering yourself morally unimpeachable. Get "fracked".

Kirsten's tiny house channel *is* a kind of documentation of a collapse. There are oodles of people fleeing to the hills, most of them white. Most of them are sick of being treated like coolies. Most of them don't know it, either. They just want an inspiring space to live in so they can get back to the bourgeois American tradition of thinking sovereign thoughts and valuing repose. Let's just say this isn't an intrinsically Mexican sensibility. In fact, lots of Hispanics will watch horror movies with the whole family like it's some kind of Family Entertainment. These are people who slaughtered one another in the millions with stone implements. No, that wasn't "statism", you spergs out there. It was an expression of identity. And so is preferring to live in an Alaskan swampland and shit in a whole in -30F weather rather than be a bugman and lose your mind in the cities. That's not "libertarianism", though libertarianism is a part of it. It's something broader and not well defined yet. But that's changing. I'm changing it. So are my friends. We're sick of this shit. Writing post-apocalyptic fiction doesn't make you a salivating sadist, an implied leftist self-manipulating over the delight of capitalism's downfall. People need to know how to act before it's too late. Many a civilization has pulled itself back from the brink through catastrophizing. And the most successful nation of them all has made its bread and butter that way. Who else but our friends in the Middle East could draw the entire world's attention onto a little girl with a journal in an attic?

BAP says you can't be grim. I'm trying not to be. It's a turnoff. I understand. All those folks in tiny homes in Idaho, Tennessee, Oregon, and northern California are just going to have a big party every day! They're not waiting for anything. They're living their lives in a more real way. There's no deeply unconscious, anticipatory component to it. They just want more time with family. They want to be less dependent on that mortgage payment. They want fewer monthly bills. That's all there is to it. They're weird and quirky! You funny liberals, embracing austerity and turning your backs on the specialization of labor the cities offer. You clearly don't understand what Ayn Rand has to say about that! People make their livings in Manhattan waiting in line for concert tickets and the latest iPhone. Can't you see this is a fact to be celebrated? What tremendous commercial diversity we've built into our society! You're "on the fringes" if you decide the white race is being openly, ethnically cleansed and you do anything other than speak up on social media for the validity of free speech. Don't be angry. Don't speak naughty words. Embrace the multicultural vibe. Transsexuals for Trump? Of course! I want my picture with that person. Who cares if the cock is pressed up right against the linen pants? There's nothing wrong here. Freedom of speech. Free expression. Free-thinking.

Men's Rights Movement

I waded my toes into "the movement" a number of years ago. I saw my most dysfunctional friends wade into Warren Farrell and pickup artistry. Never liked what I saw there. Always seemed too gentle, on the Warren end of things, or too slimy on the PUA end of things. No doubt, the struggle is real. But the solution isn't to compare men relative to women or to punish women by manipulating them into romantic scenarios.

Women and men are less comparable than they're made out to be. It could be roughly said that women have "rights". They have some avenues within the protective walls of the West, what little of them remain, through which to manifest their latent talents and abilities. Men don't have rights so much as they have patrimony, in a just society anyway. I don't want to talk about how a former feminist was led to the light by the men's rights movement. That's good for feminists. Personally, not interested. Feminism has nothing to do with our patrimony. My grandfather fought Hitler. My grandfather drove Eisenhower around in a truck and was strafed by Messerschmitts. What the fuck do I care about the documentary of some pretty, gentle woman who half the men in my "philosophical community" would give their left nut to wed? Nice lady, I'm sure. Helped a lot of people, I'm sure. But it has nothing to do with what men need to do in order to kill all the globalist pedophiles who have run our inheritances into the ground. Men need to get even with evildoers, not band together and bare their wounds over how they were divorce-raped by feminist cunts (my sympathies). Men don't group together to face women. That just frames women as having the power. Women don't have the power. Men do! Men can just punch a woman in the face. Men can do much more than that, you simply aren't allowed to talk about it publicly unless you're a faggot Communist. People forget the outsize myth of the moment, the End of The Earth titanic proportions of The Kaiser. It's not well documented in our media because that massive sense of adventure followed by the overwhelming dimensions of industrial scale slaughter is too subversive to be allowed nowadays. Don't want people getting certain thoughts in their heads. But the felt experience was there for the men we descend from. You had to have a chattier grandfather/great-grandfather or you have to wade into the archival footage to truly get a sense of it.

Here's how you don't get divorce-raped. I consulted no MRA, MGTOW, or PUA source on this because I come from a long line of sturdy farmer types who spoke their minds and kept their women. Here it is:

Never allow your woman to mother you.

Even if you're sick as hell, she fetches you the chicken noodle soup not because she's taking care of you but because you have work to do and by golly you can't just sit around on an empty stomach. Or you're worse than that, cancer or something has you bed-ridden. You have her get you the meds, the pills, whatever you need to take so you can get up on your feet and get back to doing things, by golly. Never allow a woman to drive you around. Who fucking does that? Only simps. I'm at the airport the other day and a man hugs his wife and then gets in the backseat so she can drive him home. Based, you would think. No, because she gains power over him in our modern circumstances. Women driving you around? No, only if that's their paid job and you got no relation to her. It doesn't mean women can never drive, though they do that in some places, it means that you don't let a woman drive you around. You drive around. You either drive or you submit. That's the essence of it. Also, the woman comes over to the man. Sure, the man does the initial approach. But the man does not adopt the philosophical intrigues of a single woman. That's all survival sentiments for her to appeal to a man with, it's not a lifestyle or a life's path. A woman gives that up or that's that.

And for men who are in the mouth of the beast right now, my deepest sympathies. Don't let the woman outsmart you. If she's going to be antagonistic about it or if feminism has her *enamored* with her worth, you're in the chess match of your life. You gave up your pride a long time ago. Do what it takes to be with your children but serve as a warning for men coming on down the line. Take the bitterness out of your warning. And don't remarry to some Filipina like half the fucking idiots in Montana have. Our women are the most splendid in the world. You give up first world consciousness when you dig around in the third world. If you're so cynical and self-hating about our women, maybe it's because you did it to yourself or maybe because your own mother messed up.

It's not because our women are inherently bad. Keep your sick ideology to yourself until you can dismantle it in a dispassionate setting. But Steve! feminism has ruined women in the West! Shut up. Date younger. Be more assertive. People's personalities are cast by age 27. Use that knowledge to win.

Strategy Guide Moment #3 (Up, Up, Down)

Oh boy, that one was bad. Steve was mentioned. Steve is not like that other guy. He is a silver surfer of sorts. Shoots ice beams out of his arms but not like the comic book character of a similar bent. He does it differently. His surfboard is made of whale bone, too. Fucking badass. And he takes responsibility for his life. He cleans his room. He puts his children on as many psychotropic medications as the state health system will allow. He will speak sympathetically about SSRI's while surfing around on his whale bone board. Then his daughter will fuck and cheat on her husband. He will shoot anyone who gets in her way with silver beams of ice. Don't ever fuck with this character if you get into the comedy video game. He's unstoppable. We need more people like him, unlocking minds like they do. All they ever do is unlock minds. They never ever lock minds.

What An Iconic Moment!

Jennifer Lopez's green dress is not iconic. Mainstream American culture was already poisoned to death at that point. Nothing is iconic anymore because America became multicultural in the late 1990's. The switch was made. Her green dress moment in 2000 could perhaps signify the death of American culture or its defeat by Latin America, but that is not "iconic".

America's culture died when Britney Spears' ...*Baby One More Time* was released in October of 1998 and the songwriters, producers, promoters, and performers weren't immediately placed under arrest and tried for indecency. Sure, you can peg a number of other "moments" like Tiffany in the 1980's, Michael Jackson in the early 1990's, or some of the pedophilia Jimmy Page engaged in as the death of American culture. Boomers were psyoped by VH1 and Time magazine into thinking it was the Altamont Festival in 1969 when the "sixties died" and the "fun ended". All of this shit was bad. But it was the open pedophilic nature of having Britney Spears in a short skirt girls' school outfit, making allusions to having sex/being spanked sexually one more time and the coordinated nature of the song's rise to prominence AND the fact that there weren't criminal prosecutions that America's culture died. The American Psyche broke.

That's not to say there can't be a revival, a reawakening, or that it's too late for Clive Davis to go to prison – it is simply a statement about the death of promise. This was the moment when the gatekeepers of culture turned the switch to pedophilia. A few nice moments have come out of Hollywood since but these are remnants and near-accidents, not the thrust of the culture.

There is nothing iconic in the wake of children being openly put up for sale. The main stage of this festival we are all in involves children being raped and murdered. The light show and the stage hands are all working in service of this. Sure, there may be some nice folk act on a side stage. But nobody is going to remember that. Our "festival" is wholly defined by pedophilia. There's nothing iconic about that, especially when $1/3^{rd}$ of the population is foreign born.

What would have been iconic would have been Newt Gingrich personally riding on the troop transport to Clive Davis' house and Clive's mug being paraded around in front of the cameras like they do to narcos in South America. What would have been iconic would have been for a Catholic priest to throw a shawl over Jennifer Lopez and a dedicated group of 100 young men coming to his aid to prevent law enforcement from enforcing the democratic order.

Trump winning was not iconic because the culture is still dead. It was a tremendous relief. It was unforgettable. But it was not iconic. Until there are public trials for pedophilic Hollywood, there will be little to no romance and hope in the overarching culture. There will only be acid rain.

I Don't Want To Talk About Masculinity

Don't get me wrong, it's needed in today's day and age. I talked about it some in my book *Rise And Fight*. It's a worthwhile and often lucrative topic for others to talk about. And by bringing up this framing, I'm sorta talking about it. And maybe I'll talk about it in the future. Probably not.

We have real enemies. They're cutting themselves all kinds of deals right now, even in the Trump Era. He's putting some scrutiny on them but he's pulled in a thousand different directions every day. The best laid strategy in the Beltway has been one of constant preoccupation. Hire Never Trumpers, get them to distract the President. It works but only a bit.

These enemies of ours, they are not busy taking physique pictures for other men, shilling email lists, and supplements. They are making deals. They are networking. They are reprogramming Middle America from the coasts.

Sure, you can influence the culture in a positive way by talking about masculinity. But what is to be done with the masculinity? That's the question that is never answered because the purveyor of masculinity would either be outed as a grifter fuckhead or because it would tumble the whole business down as the honest purveyor would then not be able to appear on the platforms of his fellow "tribesmen". I don't give a shit about all that. I don't need to posture and preen. Masculinity is for crushing our enemies, establishing a traditional political order, and protecting our children from globalist pedophiles. It is not a meta-pursuit in and of itself.

These midwit peddlers who distract young, insecure men from the real nature of the fight will excuse themselves by saying, "We vet each other over the Internet so that when we meet in-person we can say the things that can't be said over the Internet." Yeah fucking right. That's just a cope for a lack of courage. We need to put Hillary, Obama, Bush Jr., and their whole cabal in prison. We need to put down rioters the way they were put down by Reagan. We need stop and frisk. We need to chase "Democrats" out of our nation. We need to prosecute sexual perverts with indecency laws. We need to end the welfare state, public schools, and the Federal Reserve – and crush anyone who gets in the way. The Silent Majority needs to go into Attack Mode and viciously subdue all enemies of freedom. These aren't secrets. I'm not "spilling the beans" or "giving away intel" to the enemy. None of these masculinity gurus are actually planning anything behind closed doors that would merit the attention of the FBI. Nor am I. When the time comes, the time will come. And of course, when that time comes, I will be breaking no laws. I will be busy selling my own special line of ashwagandha pills and giving you this vital information on masculinity:

Spartan Warrior Cold Shower

Okay, men. Atten-hut! This is manosphere speaking tour veteran Has Asian Wife. The time has come for you to hit the showers. Today I'm going to be giving you a solemn, profound lecture about the Spartan Warrior Cold

Shower. During this lecture I will remember the TedX speeches I watched in preparation, ironically showing me how to gesticulate and hold eye contact. I'm funny. I teach my clients this Cold Shower all the time. This one guy, Mike Davis at 387 Crescent Drive, Sacramento, CA 95660, he pays me $250 an hour for this advice, and he has trusted me with his night urination trauma – which I am totally unprepared to deal with and so I just tell him to reprogram his negative thoughts into positive thoughts. I am his father figure. To take the Spartan Warrior Cold Shower, you need to do the following.

Step 1: Get naked.

Step 2: Turn on the cold water.

Step 3: This step is a deep secret passed on to me by my mentor, Buff Expat Who Tolerates Degeneracy. In order to unlock this manhood secret of the ages, sign up for my Members Only Facebook group for $19.95 a month. Thank you and that is all from me. (Musters best Bill Pullman Independence Day Impression) Remember, men, we are fighting for the soul of Western Civilization. Godspeed and good luck.

Man Stands At Funeral Podium

Goodbye, Mr. Congressman. You were a piece of shit your entire life. You made your city considerably worse, fucked over your black working class at every chance, substantially raised your net worth, and the *white liberal* media turned you into a folk hero because of your willingness to fuck everything in your path. I can't say I will miss you. In fact, I'm glad you're dead. I'd celebrate on social media but that would upset the conservatives who are standing in the way. If Trump was a drinker, maybe he would cut loose today and rip you a new one. Today, the day of your death. But he won't. He's not frenzied and young, like I am. I'm glad he's a stabilizing force in the world. I just wish he'd purge the grifter retards from his ranks. You were purged from the ranks by your own obesity and lack of love in your personal life. If only we had the time to wait for everyone like you to die in a hospital bed. Instead we'll have to form a coalition with the blacks, run GOP for the Latinos ad campaigns, compromise on visa deals to bring in e-verify, and forever pretend to be confused as to why Jews would vote in greater and greater proportions *against* Trump and Trumpian candidates. Yes, it's very confusing! And after all, there were *many* Jews who wrote against state expansion. Many of them! Like Murray Rothbard and Ayn Rand (both of whom eschewed their Jewish "heritage"; one to be a Catholic and one to be a Godless slut). Because they and Von Mises existed, we can never make generalizations about other people despite their overwhelming voting patterns in support of misery and Middle Eastern privation. We're supposed to be just confused about this and by asking really fucking basic questions that were answered by our listeners like 3-4 years ago, newbies to conversation will eventually be redpilled by the responses in the comment section. But of course, since we place no emphasis on making any kind of decision in society on what actually should be done, we're totally free and clear of any responsibility of anyone figuring out that hey, certain peoples aren't exactly friendly to the things America once stood for. We don't need to point out that specific waves of immigration to the United States diluted certain cultural, spiritual, and civic aspects of this once-great nation. And when others discover the truth of this and just how deep the ethnic cleansing of American whites goes and they point it out to us, we don't need to engage them publicly because those aren't stuffy asides about Plato or homosexual puff pieces about the Democratic plantation.

Yes, goodbye, black congressman. You were in the way. You doubled down. Now you are in Hell, experiencing all manner of unspeakable tortures. I hope your children lose all the money you stole and that the welfare programs they would fall back on are long gone by the time they're destitute.

Iowa Cornfield

Driving home in my 1980 F-150. It's painted barn red with a maroon side panels. The sun is just barely visible over the cornfields. I'm driving slow. The road was repaved last year, so it's a smooth ride. There are lampposts every five hundred feet or so. Pulling into my property now, up the gravel road and parking on the dirt in front of my single car garage. There were cicadas last year. Not this year. The

American flag I put in last year is waving in the breeze. I pop out of the truck and stand a minute, just listening to the quiet. I am untroubled.

People In The Way

There's not only a drunk behind the wheel but everyone else in the van is also drunk, besides you. You are the only sober one. The others are varying degrees of drunk. The most drunk is the one behind the wheel. And she's run over several people already, laughing malevolently as she did it. You're supposed to sober everyone else up by making them laugh. Funny juxtaposition, right? Haha!

Unfortunately, the drunk driver is not in a suggestible state. She is filled with bloodlust. One of these Eyes Wide Shut partygoer types. She wants this van to fuck as many people as possible before plunging like a tree chopped down by an axe. You could say she's an old battle axe. She's a proud mother. She's a civic leader. She used to be kind of pretty when she was young before the decades of moving closer and closer to the steering wheel turned her into a haggard, old witch. Now she's driving and she's angry! Point this out to everyone else. Even when she runs someone over, just keep pointing it out. We need young leaders like you. Be funny but not too funny. Be a little stodgy and clumpy. After all, the new riders in the van can't process when you get too esoteric about things. You ought never to demonstrate too deep an understanding about things. That could knock you down the rungs of the van and toward the backseat or even worse, the unventilated trailer in the back crammed with semi-living bodies.

Try not to read books on this ride. You'll get car sick. Instead listen to podcasts and watch YouTube videos only. That will keep you in the zone so you can reach as many of these drunks as possible. Who wants to learn deeper stuff anyway? Remember, keep it light and keep it funny. Even if she runs over your family, use it as rhetorical material against her. That will show them! Speak out while you have your free speech so you can save as many passengers as possible before she finally crashes the van! That's the only way. That is the most noble way. It's the most Facebook-friendly way. We're fighting for hearts and likes here.

Loveless

I think my favorite artist just gave in. Not sure. Will have to hear the rest of whatever he releases. He sings about loving yourself in this new song. That's not the worst but it's the way he does it. He makes Michael Jackson type vocalizations and the instrumentals are meant to annoy straight, white males. What a fall from grace. I saw it coming from 3-4 years out when instead of releasing a surf rock album he recorded with his buddy, he released an album honoring a local female artist who does stupid, untalented shit. And he started dating a single mom not long before that. And one of the songs he sings on the album is about how he adores how she will never allow herself to be tied down. That's my interpretation. Could be about himself but it leads to the same thing: dead atomization.

Ironic that a man singing about loving himself signals the death of his good years. Doesn't always work out that way but a lot of the times it does. Why? Loving yourself is almost always a leftist mantra that people repeat to themselves after they've done a bit of therapy. There's nothing wrong about loving yourself but you have to be a good person in order for there to be love. You can't just be a degenerate and "love yourself". All that does is give you internalized moral sanction to ruin society, one little act at a time. Some things are inherently evil, some are inherently good. We love what is good and we reject what is evil. Leftist psychologists don't posit it that way. They say to discover what's there and just love it no matter what. But that's not the same as appreciating what's there and nurturing it, whether through sternness or compassion, until it is healthy and sane once again. The leftist psychologist imbues in her clients the equivalent of running around a prison, hugging everyone and doing a little bit of drugs with them. When an artist internalizes these standards, he loses touch with the flicker of madness that drove his pre-self-aware life. He becomes an ideology. The flicker of madness in him was masculine. Now he has become the toxic feminine. Tragic. Psychotherapy may stabilize people out of their addictions but it also ruins the artistry of men. Men are even allowed to be "champions" by psychology but only in endeavors that are non-exclusionary. Discrimination must not be viewed as a positive. Discrimination is always prejudiced, pathological, and harmful to the oppressed. Thus, man is a sports champion or a corporate champion. This kills true artistry. Artistry deals with fury. Modern psychology is meant to stamp it out.

How To Be Nice To People

Seeing this news article about Shaq donating a year's rent to a shooting victim's mother so she doesn't have to put her disabled son through homelessness. That's *nice*. Avowed. The woman is black and so is her son. Did this garner her any extra sympathy? Probably. Shaq, in his heyday, was one of the earlier examples of a black athlete investing his money responsibly – for the most part. He owns a bunch of restaurants, gobs of real estate, and who knows what else. He produces a healthy income stream, to say the least, from his phenomenal basketball career earnings. Can't fault the man for doing so. Materially, he has a good life.

Remember that kid in the Minnesota mall (was it Minnesota?) who was thrown from a third floor balcony, landed on hard concrete on the first level, and practically died? White kid. Terrible medical bills. The savage who did that to him is in prison, at least for a while. I sent money to help that kid and his parents cover the medical bills. I'd do it again. Because he was white and because the white race is being ethnically cleansed, I'm more sympathetic. I've sent money to a number of people who have had their causes championed by conservatives, not all of them white. But most. And who are we kidding, whites make up the majority of conservatives on the planet.

I enjoy being nice to people. I'm only grouchy on the Internet or while driving. Thinking of that fuckhead who changed lanes right in front of me going 10 miles under the speed limit while I was going the exact perfect limit (since I never ever break the law and neither should you) and had the nerve to flip me off twice and then proceeded to pace the other car in the other lane, both going 10 miles under the speed limit. Let's just say I wanted to tickle fight that guy. Pillow fight! We'd step out of our vehicles, he in his Kia Sonata and me out of my truck, our blood pumping, and proceed to wail on each other with feather pillows. What tremendous fun! How philosophical of me. Yes, driving is fun when the average person is 40 IQ points dumber than you and dropping like a rock because 1/6th of our population is illegals. Being grouchy on the Internet? Being grouchy in my books? Is it grouchy, though? Or is everyone in the fucking way all the fucking time and The Great Slowdown is real? Sure, I could habituate myself to the Slowdown and calmly and kindly explain philosophical principles till I'm blue in the face. I'm willing to do that. Still do it. But can't a guy hammer down on his V8, pass some shitprick with California plates, and bomb down the hill going the exact speed limit like a Boy Scout of old? The speed limit. It's important. So are red lights. You must always stop for those. You must wait and wait.

Here are the things you need to slow down for in this life:

-women who are nervous

-stoplights

-third world medical professionals

-Silicon Valley vampires

-people who are less smart than you

That's how you be nice. Being nice has nothing to do with breaking away from the pack, leaving everyone in your dust and going fast, fast, fast. If you do that, then everyone is entitled to shoot arrows into your back until you die like some Medieval wolf cornered in the forest by some hungry Romanian peasants. Be nice. Never ever become impatient. Never speak with too much urgency in your voice. Never make fun of or counter-signal others in your tribe that are *fucking slow* and in the way, especially the nervous women. Never lose your patience ever for any reason because that's your False Self and you need to breathe deeply because when you're relaxed, you're at your best. That's what Elie Wiesel told himself in the concentration camps and look what happened to him. He won some big prizes! Champion of the ages. Influential psychologist. You should especially never express impatience publicly because that's "accelerationism"

and since the midwits who are in your periphery can't
tolerate their own feelings of impatience for any real length
of time, you are being unphilosophical. You can write, think,
and feel this way without using stimulants and you will be
blamed for abusing stimulants, so don't even think about it,
Buster.

In the Medieval Age, there were speed limits. You
couldn't run too fast. You couldn't upset nervous women.
You obviously had Saracen doctors who *loved* you and
tended to your illnesses (remember, they were astronomers,
nuclear engineers, and autist level mathematicians before the
mean other-Muslims rode in and slaughtered them all).
People who were less smart than you were never ever tossed
aside when expedient. Everyone was together, one big happy
family. That's the way it is now. That's the way it has always
been but Trump threatens to derail it all. He and the white
supremacists.

Coombrain

Bro, don't coom. Bruh. Keep your grey matter, bruh.
I see you, isolating yourself. You think no one cares. Or you
don't care that I care. Or you think that I will shame you for
cooming. Not into that. You think that when we leave the
house that the scrutiny is off of you. You think that you
won't know. But you do know. You know when you give
yourself coombrain, even if you can't admit to yourself. We'll

see it. We'll see how you've become depressed. We'll watch you twitch, fidget, and doubt yourself. We'll see your belly fat pile up. We'll see you skip workouts. We'll see you cheat with carbs. We'll see you use old jokes you've already used. We'll see you lose your resistance to female persuasions. We'll see you make sexual Rick and Morty type jokes. You'll find potty humor to be funnier. You'll have this self-detonating way of speaking that cuts you. You'll build up all these judgments in your head that you anticipate we have of you. You'll undermine yourself before we've even said a word. You'll gripe about how you're so addicted. That this is the worst addiction of your life. That you don't want to hang out with us as much because you're not worthy.

But it's very simple: don't coom.

That's the ticket to heaven. That's the pathway to creativity. That's what puts you in good with the women you crave. When you don't coom, your power levels build up. Your strength comes back. The longer you've been a habitual coomer, the more days in a row of not cooming until your headspace clears and improves. The doctors won't tell you this. Often, they will tell you the opposite. They'll tell you that it's the body's natural function to coom every two weeks to a month. That if you don't coom, you will have problems with your balls. Your stool will change! This is preposterously bad and so therefore, when did a little Internet porn hurt anyone. The world's greatest philosopher told me that once. We all make mistakes. He was probably on coombrain. We're in this struggle together. Bruh, don't coom. There's doom in the coom. The hormonal wash turns you into a slave. It activates your self-debt (typo, it's self-doubt but self-debt is more fitting), no matter how much you deny it to us. We know. We know when you've been wicked. We know when non-Euro coomers are training themselves to take our women. It's abundantly apparent. Hey, embrace *the way* – they say. But we know better. We are the keepers of the bloombrain… or whatever you want to call it. The pineal gland tradition. Something along those lines. Whatever it is, it is the absence of coombrain. Complete absence. Takes a long time to get to. Neural pathway healing over time. That's the ticket. Don't put too much pressure on yourself. Don't be foul to yourself. That will only put you in the coom realm. Hungry, angry, lonely, tired? Careful you don't coom. Remember the healing over time. Heal your brain, bruh.

A Philosophical Poem

I can refer to whites without meaning, "Every single white person."

I can refer to Jews without meaning, "Every single Jew all of the time forever."

I can refer to blacks without meaning, "Every single black person."

What's your response? Not all Jews!

Heavens above, get the fuck out of my way. Why are you in the way?

(super nefarious 50's Batman supervillain voice) Yes, every single person of that ethnic group. Bwahaha!

(105 IQ Steve Crowder mug club voice) Step aside, evildoer! I have come to defeat you with facts and logic. Not ALL of that ethnic group. En garde!

105 IQ Steve Crowder Mug Club Voice

Being gay is funny! Asians are funny! Ching chong. I'm witty, like Starlord from Guardians of the Galaxy. But I'm also kind of edgy. I am a programmer. But I also lift weights. Deus Vult, brother! We are going to save the West with individualism. Get out of my way, far right. You are all racists and you are not funny. I am funny, like Starlord from Guardians of the Galaxy. Jorden Peterson voice: I am Groot! My wife gave me a little something-something last night, if you know what I mean. She thinks I'm funny. She laughs in my face loudly when we are having fun. Vote for Trump! But hesitate because he's a boor. Didn't vote for him last time. That's okay. My power levels have risen. Ben Shapiro? He's a turd. Duh! Pouring myself a glass of wine now, thank you. There's actually a huge shared space between metal music and conservatism. I'm a visionary. Burp! Fixing my bowtie now. I'm a little quirky like that. Me and my girlfriend-wife like to go bowling. But we're a little uncomfortable when non-white people are there. Just a little. Forget I ever said that. Oops. My wife is burping in my face. She's hilarious. She's laughing hysterically. That's cause she's in the Mug Club with me. We are libertarians, at heart. We want to homeschool our kids. I'm going to make my kids laugh so hard. They're gonna be such little goobers. We are going to raise them to be individuals. Slay the dragon! Hey bro, don't make fun of black people, okay? Black people make fun of white people. White people…what does that even mean? We're all distinct from each other. Remember, white people come from different countries. And the metal music from those different countries is distinct. Oops, I jerked off again. Better not tell a single soul about that.

Secretly, I hope my favorite superheroes jerk off in private. Thor got fat because he watched too much milf porn. Starlord is sardonic because he warms up to porn and then his wife finishes him off, like me. If you tell anyone, I'll just pretend like you never existed. In fact, it was you who wronged me. You are far right. You abuser. You are not libertarian at heart. You make these awful generalizations that offend my metal-honed sensibilities. Look at you, you are self-defeating. Just chill and smoke a cigarette with my wife while she eyes you lustily. Oh, going out for a second. Gotta get some CBD and some wine. Don't cuck me, bro. I'm not a closeted homosexual. Homos are funny! See how I said homo? Anyway, be right back. Oops, forgot my vape pen. Let me say that again louder but in a clown voice because I'm funny. My wife was showing you my rare guitar collection I bought with my coding money? Yeah, this one is green like a green screen. Okay, I'll be back in a second. (Please don't see the bottle of lotion next to the computer or my wife's period streaks in the underwear she leaves strewn about our bedroom floor next to my rare guitar collection).

Back with some wine and laughs. Glad you guys saved a spot for me on the couch. This Silicon Valley marathon is going to be EPIC! These guys are fucking hilarious. I'm laughing and now my wife is laughing in my face, three inches away. I feel her spit peppering me. I don't give a fuck if you're bored or not because we're bros. We became forever bros when you let me crash on your couch when my wife almost left me because…oh, I'm not supposed to talk about that. Then you might get the drift of who I really am. Don't worry, I jerk off just like you. We're fine. But I'm a little different, a little edgy. A libertarian, at heart. Can't wait to own some acres and raise the little ones. First, I have to murder my wife's soul.

Strategy Guide Moment #4

You know that sound children make when they are on the verge of constipation and are straining to get the poop out of themselves. Uhhh. You know the sound.

That's the only sound that comes out of Andrew Yang's mouth. Actually, he's so completely forgettable that unless he gets clubbed under his left eye by Oprah, nobody will remember who he is in a year's time. Let's just say he's

Oriental. One of the mini-bosses. A libertarian, at heart. He will stand in your way, especially if you bring urbanized, deracinated sensibilities into his realm. Then he will hammer you with *Math*. Just dodge. Then point out how he is Oriental to his face. Don't be racist about it. State it as a matter of fact.

Walking With Champions

Hello, my apprentice. We have been friends for years now. I, the master. You, the apprentice. I have come to deliver the good word of the Champion. You don't like the Champion because your mind is ruined. That's okay. I will give you the insight, bud. The insight is that we must walk like titans. Our every step must shake the forest trees. The snow will shake from their branches as we stomp through. We have the vibrational force of our forefathers. We are soulful and we understand Europa. Hyperion! Rise, o voices of Europa. We're turning our movement into a movement of warmth and nobility, goy. Now I am laughing like a nobleman. The word goy is funny because its use connotes my advanced knowledge of the situation at hand. Hail, victory!

We'll have to start our own conference where everyone has the spirit of Europa. Our volkenwomen will have braids in their hair and though I beat the tar out of my woman, I am still a leader of this volkenmarsch. Wow, nice fashy haircut, brother. If I were a homosexual, I would be in a Spartan legion with you and we would bathe in the natural springs. I would violently take you in the brush while our troop was resting on the eve of battle. We would cuddle after the fact, steeped in our deep wisdom together. These are not those times, however my apprentice, and you have a thick mustache now. You are a lawyer. Together we make a great team. Me with my aristocratic bearing and you with your racial hatred and thinly veiled hyper-rage. Why does everyone block us on Twitter? It's because we have the *facts*. They're weak. You are my phalanx, apprentice. You are the striking force. I am the warlock in the high tower, crafting the deep harmonies that will free our people forever.

One False Move

She's looking to kill you. She knows how to do it. She will try. You must hold fast. Don't give in. Give her the illusion you've given in, even. But don't give in. Stay locked in. Do it the right way. You can flirt with oblivion just to spite her. To show her that you are far more in command than she is. She is the destroyer. You've met her before. Too many times. This is her naivety. She thinks you haven't met one like her before. She won't push it as far as she thinks she will have. She's fishing for the final evidence. She will team up with whoever she has to and you know it. You can sense it. The thought scares you because you want to believe in the good in her. That's the pull. That's her power. You want to believe in her good. You will find that it's long gone. You know that already, so hold strong. Don't give an inch. She's waiting for one false move. She's just the female version of this. She has more power than the others who do this. You are still young. You can fight fire with fire, if it comes down to it. Whoever said you can't is a stupid pushover who succumbed. No, see how far into the dance she can push you. There's the thrill in it. You know. That's why I won't stop you outright. You have to let the conflict have a deadly aspect to it so that you'll be pushed to new heights. In a sense, it's wonderful. But not to her. It's agony the whole way. Don't let her get you, D'Artagnan. She'll bring whoever she needs to into it once you've given her the foothold she needs.

When she gets others in, they will play less nimbly. They will wreck whatever they can. That's the actual danger. If she was totally alone, there would be no danger. But no woman is alone anymore. Not any smart ones, anyhow. She knows the power she has over you. It's just not enough. But she doesn't know that. She won't know it until she breaks, until her own wickedness suffocates her. She'll deny it until her death but you will see the truth.

Soften Up

Soften up now, bud. You're a father, after all. I'm a father, too. Hold on, my wife is saying something to me. Just one more second. Okay, back. Sorry about that. Did you know that studies show that a man's testosterone drops by up to 50% upon being around his first-born child? That happened to me. It happened to you, too, bud. We're the Old Guard now. We've got to show these young fellas a gentler way. Remember, the state wants to gets its hands on the young, disaffected youth in order to put them through the meatgrinder of totalitarian ideologies. We are the wizened patriarchs holding back the tide of chaos.

Hold on, my wife needs something. Alright, I'm back. Studies show that men are looking for their careers to improve while women are looking for a sense of security. Yeah, that's what they show. It's time for us to soften up but just a tiny bit. For example, I am still powerlifting. Nothing like deadlifting to AC/DC, am I right? Tell your son this. Look at us, a couple of patriarchs. But you, you're going a little too hard, brother. Studies show that your heart health increases in importance as you age and after all, you're in your thirties now. Heart disease is the number one killer of men. I know, I did that Heart Walk last month. We should run a 5k sometime. I bet I can run it faster than you just like I can deadlift a little bit more than you. A bit of friendly rubbing between two fathers, right? Studies show that male loneliness is an epidemic right now. If you ever need to reach out to me, I will counsel you, brother. After all, I am a bit older than you and more experienced as a father. Take it easy with that political stuff. We need to focus on building a legacy for ourselves, our tribe. You know what my favorite drink is? Scotch on the rocks. It's a classy drink. I'm classy. I clean up nice. I'm a businessman. You have a lot you can learn from me. I am going to teach you the things your father never taught you. You're a father now, after all. Welcome! Welcome to the Father's Club (came up with that one myself). Okay, our time is up. That'll be 150 dollars. Thanks, bud. Secret father's salute! See you next week or on social media in a minute.

Self-Checkout

Taxpayer ID #4093819: Hello, sir. Right this way. I'm watching you intensely. Yes, sir, you have to put it on the table there. I don't know why. It's just part of the process. Not like in our day. That's funny! Television. TV dinners. Okay, you can put that one back in your cart. I have the override key here. Done. Now you hit Finish & Pay. Yeah, put the card in there. Chip readers, right? Not like in our day. Lost In Space. The moon landing. Now remove the card. Good, you got it. Takes a while to get used to, huh? The cashback comes out from down there. Funny, right. Okay, sir, you have a wonderful day. Thanks for shopping with us.

Oligarch Charlie Kirk: You, buddy. Yeah, sorry to bother you. Who is that on the screen there? 4093819, you say? Alright, send her in. Gorsh, I can't help but feel sorry for her.

Taxpayer ID #4093819 (entering the office): Mr. Kirk, what an honor. I didn't know you were touring our store today. I loved you in that one thing.

Kirk: Please, Taxpayer ID #4093819, call me "Charlie". Everyone, please leave the room. I'd like to speak to Taxpayer ID #4093819 alone.

Great, look, I think you're doing a fantastic job at the self-checkout aisle. You're one of our best employees. Employee of the month last year, I see from your file. That's fantastic. Look, I know I said I was going to be giving you some training. In fact, you'd be one of our great black revolutionaries – breaking other blacks out of the Democratic plantation. The thing is, we found someone who can do your job better than you. Taxpayer ID #4093819, please meet ChinaBot 400.

ChinaBot400: *beeps a greeting consisting of three tones*

Taxpayer ID #4093819: Oh, Mr. Kirk-

Kirk: Please, call me Charlie.

Taxpayer ID #4093819: Yes, okay. Look, I worked really hard to get this job. I beat out 250 other applicants. I need this job. I haven't missed a day in the 16 months I've been working here.

Kirk: That's right. Your record is flawless. I'm sorry, I just hate to do this. ChinaBot 400 is the way of the future. Please understand, if I don't replace you with ChinaBot – I myself will be replaced. It's just my job, ma'am. I'm sorry. But look, I care about the black community. African-American unemployment is at an all-time low. Jobs! This is what I can do for you: I can offer you a volunteer position as a brand ambassador black revolutionary who breaks Democrats off of the black plantation. Whoops. Got that wrong! I mean, you will be a black breaking other blacks off of the Democrat plantation. If you are a good brand ambassador and are never ever pictured with someone you shouldn't be associating with and as long as you never say an ill word about Israel, I will eventually be in the position to offer you a $45k a year job. Not bad for a woman without a college education, huh?!

Taxpayer ID #4093819: Charlie, I can't begin to thank you enough. This is a huge break for me and Israel. Tell your 100% free market, Randian bosses that I will take the position at once. I am the new Harriet Tubman.

Kirk: Indeed, you are. Let me get a picture of us smiling together with the other African-Americans nearby. (Calls everyone together). Everyone, smile! Thanks, everyone. You are all my friends. Taxpayer ID #4093819 is my latest friend. You all are coming to the No Whites Allowed Conference next month, correct? I knew you were. You are my deepest friends.

Taxpayer ID #4093819: Charlie, I see a little Chinese man stepping out of the back of that robot. I thought it was a robot that was replacing me. I'm confused, y'all.

Kirk: Taxpayer ID #4093819, please be careful. "Y'all" is a word that our corporation prefers we not be seen saying in public. As a brand ambassador, you are going to have to be better.

Taxpayer ID #4093819: Yes, Charlie. I submit to your wisdom, which you learned from PragerU. But please, tell me why there is a Chinese man now smoking a cigarette next to the fake robot.

Kirk: Ah, you've got me there. I hope we can still be friends. Please promise me your friendship before I give an explanation. My lawyer is here now, in a flash, and he is ready to get your signature so that if you hurt our friendship, I can litigate like John Galt did. Okay, now that our business contract is signed and we are friends, I will tell you why there is a Chinese man inside a fake robot suit. The truth is that he's here LEGALLY. He came here on a visa. Some of my favorite Senators who I know personally signed off on the bill that brought him here. Legal immigration is cool.

Taxpayer ID #4093819: I guess you're right. I accept my role as brand ambassador and I don't care about my old job. Can I please put in my Twitter bio that I am associated with you?

Kirk: Yes, please do. Okay, see you later! Money bless you.

Repossession

The average Millennial makes somewhere around $40k (state by state is much lower), according to a recent infographic I saw on Twitter. I'm not going to cite it because this is four days after the fact and nobody younger than me cares all that much since this figure lines up with most people's experience anyway: Millennials make way less than Boomers and their life expectancy has gone down, for the first time in American history. I would wager to guess that Zoomers have it even worse. We know the bankers, lobbyists, Congressmen, feminists, Third Worlders, Commie professors, and bureaucratic elite are doing this. The dispossession itself is crushing. I feel for the people of my generation. I have eked out a life for myself out of nearly a decade of sheer workaholism (my five years of college largely kept me out of the workforce and kept me distracted). Workaholism, grind, whatever you want to call it. That and I have a higher than average IQ than the average American. What a gift a higher IQ is. Combined with clear thinking, it gives you the ability to make up for lost time. And when the Great Slowdown is occurring without your consent, there's time to make up for even if you've been at your absolute best for years in a row. Your time is being stolen because the currency is being inflated, there's government gridlock everywhere, and there's no freedom of association. We've been over some of this.

To my wagies out there, save your money or reinvest it into yourself. I have a 50% savings rate currently. It's never dipped below 25% in the past three years. Sometimes it's as high as 70% but only rarely and usually only on a more profitable month where my bills are lower. I get hammerfucked by taxes like three times a year. Gotta save up for that shit. Giving up is seductive but it's only viable in the short run. When you persevere, eventually it gets better. But it takes at least the better part of a decade. Saving as much money as you can helps. I hurt my knee 11 months ago and had to take time off of work. I couldn't walk without hopping around for 3 weeks. I had money saved up, just in case. Right now, I'm saving for unforeseen circumstances. It's just better this way.

Investing in yourself can run the gamut from getting therapy with a non-shitlib therapist (some of the shitlib therapists are decent, I'll give them that), paying for a subscription or monthly donation to a content creator that is helping you, gym membership, buying books that you read (my main extravagance), giving money every week to your non-globo homo church, buying a better bed so you sleep better, or upping the nutrition content of your groceries. I'd say tinkering with supplements is useful but if you're eating a good diet, there's really no need for them. At best, you may see a short-term performance bump. At worst, you become weird and overly convinced of their effect. Lots of weirdos hawking supplements out there who'd be happier sourcing their own meat or buying from a local butcher.

College is a scam, by and large. There'd better be a clear path to a good-paying scheme or none of it is worth it. The trades are good. Hard sciences are better. Computer stuff is a hot ticket. Entrepreneurship is not for the faint of heart but if you can make it work, make it work. Nothing like being your own boss. Nothing like serving people directly and seeing the rewards in real-time. One of the best things we have going in the West is the ability to go into business for yourself and other than not being able to turn people away unless they're actively aggressive toward you, we have some freedom. That's the basic freedom though, isn't it? Turning people away because you simply don't like them.

My heart goes out to my Zoomer and Millennial compatriots. Not everyone is going to make it. Some of us will be pulled under. It's dog eat dog. I didn't want it this way. I don't make it this way. I try to make it the opposite. I support our guys and I put my money where my mouth is. No handouts, of course. Only when a kid is in the hospital, like I mentioned earlier. Maybe it's better that it's dog eat dog for a while. The cream will rise to the top? Not if we're legally dispossessed. We live in interesting times. The online army is assembling. You can feel it. You can feel the culture tilting, bit by bit. The faggotry of the left, the managerial elite, and the third world is being made fun of at every turn. We're sick of this shit.

$40k doesn't get you much. It doesn't get you a $350k house, which is the average cost of one now. It hardly gets you rent on the coasts. You're just barely out of the ghetto on $40k (which is taxed) and that's with roommates. Meanwhile, foreign kids here on their parents' NAFTA/WTO swindle money live in luxury and steal our women. Not allow. The Third Worlders are worse in Europe. They just walk in and start raping. But our demographics are much less intact. Few Colonial Stock strains having any success. Too much autism. Too much programmed self-loathing. Castizos and Medis are ascendant, though I don't count out the Teutons. The ascendant ones are the vigorous ones with the IQ to make the difference. We'll pray for our Anglos, won't we? $500 a week gets you a cot in a garage, the aching feeling that the groceries you're buying aren't giving you what you need, and the constant stress of worrying about what the next car repair will be. You've got to branch out. Read more books. Talk to more people at work. Associate with people who are more valuable than you. That's the deal. That's the recipe. I didn't charge you $300 an hour to be told that. Write down the recipe on a piece of paper and post it somewhere you will see it, over and over until you *actually* internalize it:

```
-Branch out more

-Read more books

-Talk to more people at work

-Associate with people who are more valuable
than you
```

When you get stuck, talk to different people. Don't read books you think you *ought* to read. Read what is profitable and what is inspiring. Check the inside text before you buy so you know you can actually flow with the prose. Don't get bogged down in slogs unless it's a highly technical read that translates to real world dollars (like a book on coding). If you start to not like your friends, gracefully take your space and make new friends. Remember that loyalty matters for something in the long run and keeping up appearances is what people have done for eons. That's it. $300 of coaching in like two paragraphs. Notice how I keep my stuff affordable to the wagies. Remember my loyalty to you when you end up making more money. Always put our guys over the top. I look out for you; You look out for me.

This is how I climbed out of the government job, miserable marriage, mainstream media path that I was set to walk. There's nothing cynical about it. I am basically conventionally unemployable unless one of our guys is willing to give me something quiet on the side, and personally I'd prefer to just keep doing this work. I like the hunt. I ate boiled eggs for years "for my art." I quit jobs that to outsiders looked like the decision-making of a "flake" or a crazy person, just to stay in the hunt. I outlasted psychic vampires, philosophical bullies, creepy invasive weirdos, brutal landlords, smokestack hyper cities, nauseating plane flight after nauseating plane flight, gatekeepers (they do exist, just in fewer numbers than purported), Big Tech censorship, actual stalkers, Hillary Clinton throwing a planet-sized bitch fit, my financial investments mercilessly kicking me in the balls repeatedly, getting dropped by a bank because of my political beliefs, and a bunch of other crazy shit. The ideas in this book are not allowed. I am not allowed. But I persist because I believe the best is yet to come. We can have another golden age but not until we get these impish paper-pushers out of the way. They're dug in!

Keep going.

Strategy Guide Moment #5

Hello, Boomer. You have been reading this book in the hopes of gaining some brilliant insight into "the enemy" but it doesn't work that way. You don't know it, though, because you see things in the old way. You're fucking terrified by half of what is in this book. Conjures up images of a dangerous professor hard at work deep in the woods. Your terror is pathetic. You're not happy to ride off into the sunset sipping margaritas and popping $15 headache pills. No, you want The Final Showdown. How boring. We don't have any time to accommodate you. We have to "stick with it". You don't understand that. You think you do and you feel hatred. Not the vibe. Sorry, guy.

Saying "No" To Cringe

Some people are cringe. Their interpersonal skills are defined by the hyperautism they went through in childhood and so when they try to relate, they fumble and fail. But it's worse than that, they dull the people they engage in. Most of it is isn't malicious, it's just gawky and uncomfortable. But it doesn't matter because the sum effect is to dull others into their own worldview instead of vibing. Say "no" to people who are cringe.

Vibing is the opposite of cringe. Vibing requires high IQ, high awareness, and the hunger to want it badly enough. What is *it*? The vibe. You can only vibe if you're constantly stripping away all the bullshit. Someone pointed out that I wrote a line of cringe in a book of mine a few years back. I immediately disavowed. Sorry, Jesus. I may have written it but I am vibing more than I was then.

The cringe can learn to vibe but they're not your burden or your concern. They can jailbreak themselves from their current levels of cringe with self-knowledge and with riding the tiger. But they will probably never be able to hang with you. This is why it's so important to never coom, to never indulge addictions, and to always listen to the prophesizing voice inside yourself. Follow the genius who unburdens you. Don't be cringe, bro. Don't hold on to what is killing you. Don't shove it onto others' plates and then tantrum when you aren't well received. If you aren't well-received by the people who are vibing, re-adjust privately and try to ride the wave again. If you're enough of a distraction, people who are vibing will point out your autism but not as a favor to you. They'll do it because you're an example of what not to do. Some guys do this kindly and gently. Some do it with fury. Everyone has their own style. Be true to yourself, bro. Don't just copy the style of people who are vibing. That's not how it works. Others can only serve as guideposts; you have to do the walking yourself.

If you post cringe, try to live with it. Just get better. It's not always easy. We all hit slumps. We're human. Sometimes you need to delete your cringe. I've seen guys who are vibing take down whole swaths of cringe. Some of it is on the Internet forever and you just live with it. But cringe is not acceptable, either. Remember, there are other people who are trying vibe. Get out of their way!

A big cringe trap is people who try to be funny but aren't funny. Funny is the intersection between madness and truth. It's a discipline but also an embodied state. Don't just fling shit out there and expect it to stick. Yet, that's how it works for the masters. That's cause they're dialed in. They're vibing. You're not going to be funny to people who are vibing if you have the following:

-obesity

-a vagina (exception is daughters making their fathers laugh or wives being feminine in a disarming way to their husbands: this can never be encapsulated in a stand-up routine)

-passé political stances

-coombrain

-a need to be liked and accepted (take care of that privately, bruh)

-too much suspicion of the people near you

There are others but that's a good start. Remember, people younger than you are less indoctrinated in the shit you had to go through by virtue of the fact that communication has opened up in the interim and the good ones in their ranks have watched you make your mistakes. The youth movement is never cringe. The young men without families have the least chance of being cringe. Learn from them.

Big Tent

Trump 2020. Trump Successor 2024. Operation Send Them Home. Operation Bring Them Home. America First. That's the big tent. There are cringe people under this tent. There are women. There are smart people, dumb people, beautiful and ugly. It's a big tent. Our guys get chased out by the security guards.

Grifters, Inc.

Grifters are a thing. It's not some "leftist" slur meant to malign people who are seeking profit. Exploitation is a real thing, despite what some people would tell you about usury. Usury is voluntary! Yeah, okay, let a 160 IQ Foreigner push pornography onto a vulnerable, susceptible 95 IQ population. That's voluntary! Those people, stripped of their religion and dumbed down with chemicals, can *choose* not to look at the porn. Ignore the lifelong damage that's already been done. People who prey on the dumb by defrauding them with rapacious loans are just behaving in the spirit of capitalism. China defrauding the entire continent of Africa is *totally* different from the principle of usury because GOVERNMENT is involved! It's not like people guilty of usury have the intellectual means to help their fellow man get help in a sustainable way. There's no opportunity cost there. There's no other decision they could make. They're just free market anarcho-capitalists providing market needs. If you speak out against them, you are a red book carrying Marxist who hates capitalism! Christianity is cool so long as it keeps together families but when it forbids usury, it's antiquated and non-anarcho-philosophical and we just quietly forget that part so that we can stay allied with our Christian friends in the culture war.

When an e-girl shows off the swell of her breasts to a generation of lonely men starving for existential purpose, that's the free market! Her tiddies are libertarian at heart. She has it hard! Life is difficult for her. She does not have other options. She can't do like Faith has done and keep those things to herself. When some squat little woman flashes her chest-vipers built up from eating too many vegetable carbs from the diet that brings her attention from lonely men on the Internet, you are supposed to graciously thank Capitalism that there's a place for women in our movement. The lonely men destroyed by three generations of divorce and feminism are *voluntary* simps and we must place the entire burden of change on them because we are being consistent here with respect to the principle. E-girls who flash tiddies are the same as usurers but we can wiggle out of that on some psychological technicality having to do with childhood trauma. Any sort of mental gymnastics to keep the moneylenders going. Moneylending and debt are part of the free market, bro. A people are only truly free when they've paid homage to the brave lenders charging exorbitant interest rates that were previously banned by societies far more Christian than ours. Oh, come on! Usury is not a thing, bro. It's voluntary, bro. Clean that Karl Marx out of your head. Usury was never a concept that predated the French Revolution. The banning of usury never led to better conditions for the peasant and more evenly distributed incomes. The banning of usury cannot be morally justified because the entire transaction is voluntary. Can someone open my bottle of Dream Poison for me? I am choosing to drink this Dream Poison. I am a voluntary society personified.

Scorpion Neck

When we were both 17, a guy in my neighborhood I used to play in bands with got a tattoo of a scorpion on his neck. I remember asking him if he was sure he wanted a scorpion on his fucking neck when he was 80. Dude was troubled. His father was absent, wealthy.

He said yes. Then there was a scorpion on his neck. Then he got Rage Against The Machine stars on his wrists.

It's wild to think that the time to get through to him was probably when he was 17. To think that maybe the majority of people are that way. That these spiritual/moral compromises stack up early and HEAVY.

I reached out to the guy maybe 5 years ago. He was initially receptive but then ghosted me. I had the distinct sense it was because of my politics, my moral stance. He didn't want to be JUDGED. Probably picked it up from his single mom, who dated/married around.

People hate having judgment passed on them. I understand why. Makes them feel exposed. When you're highly traumatized but try to keep some artistry going, you are fragile. Another person's moral conscience is like a wrecking ball coming through. Leftism is a glass house but it's built on social ostracism. I had the sense that not only was it his need not to be judged but it was also his wife's politics that pushed me out of his life for good. Her politics were based in the ugly things she had done with her life. And the ugly things her parents had done to her, even just psychologically. I understand how unbearable it would be to try to be friends with someone who has a knowledge of a lot of your suffering, because it's clearly on display, and have to face your own unwillingness to change – every time he came around. No fun. Better to socially ostracize the guy so you can normalize.

Drifting Off

Fogginess is a hell of a coping mechanism. Don't make me grow! Don't make me think! People spend years sedating themselves. There's a woman nursing a Ben &

Jerry's ice cream tub, a hefty glass of wine, and a *Friends* marathon because college left her surrounded by feminists. There's a guy surfing the Internet with coombrain for a fourth hour in a row. The cloud descends and the inner life is muted.

Boredom is a bit different. Too often the same but there's a special kind of boredom that comes from being crushed by the Slowdown. Your avenues to success are siphoned off. Your ability to foster stimulating conversations is inhibited from without. The content that comes out is rehashed crap because few people take real chances. That boredom is understandable. We've got guys working on that.

The fogginess is the killer. Not for you and I, I would assume. But maybe we'd be surprised. Guys have a fatigue with the concepts. They turn to douchebag centrists for emotional comfort. "I was listening to so-and-so but he's just so boring," is either valid because you're chasing the bleeding edge or it's invalid because you're afraid of conflict and need an excuse to wiggle back to comfort. It's a killer. You can do a whole host of things out of your fogginess. You can become a gymcel. You can play music too loudly on your Beats for too long and just not notice. You can be too online. You can chase the Everlasting Mama. You can fight with Online Papa. You can waste time at a dead-end job (yes, they do exist). You can move out of America or Canada and live in some 2nd world comfort zone. You can tip even though the service was bad. The fogginess is there for you. Drowsiness is ready and waiting.

Stay awake during the day. Sleep 7-9 hours at night.

e-girls

If you need to show me your boobs, I don't care
what you have to say…especially if you already have a man
in your life. It's one thing to be prowling about for a man. I
can *kind of* understand that. But not really. If you have a nice
figure, it'll show in a full sweater. That's the truth.

I get that it's a business strategy. Sex sells. Known
that since forever. But I think you're showing off your tits as
a show of power. I don't give a fuck if you're a libertarian
peaceful parent who's been through five years of
psychotherapy. You're still showing off your tits. There's still
something fucked up about you. You want to prey on men.
There's something wrong in your relationship to men.
Especially if you're irreligious or disrespect Christianity by
not giving it its due. Then nobody has a foothold in with you
other than your man and if he's willing to tolerate his woman
using her chest weapons to gain clout, then he's not strong
and probably likes you because of your fucked-up
relationship to men.

You may get all the attention in the world from
simps but the only attention you're going to get from me is
my immediate disgust reaction to your spiritual sickness.
When you take down your shitty profile picture with you
wearing cheap lipstick and your pumped-up fat deposits,

then maybe I will consider some compassion for whatever trauma you went through that makes you want to take your revenge on men. Until then, you are weaponized. Damnation upon you. I was raised by modest people, I am married to a modest woman, I have only dated modest women. You're not here to influence me. The more likes your stupid tweets get, the more turned off by you I become. You only exist to me because openly attacking you for your abuse of men is a distraction from the way things need to go. You will be dealt with, in time. Enough of us will figure out that you're a sick twit and we'll tune you out! Haha! Then it will all be resolved, won't it? That's how our leaders say it works. But it won't work out that way. You'll still be fucked up. You'll still have a simp as a boyfriend-husband. And you'll still give your ice-cold takes on social media and simps will lap it up because there's a never-ending supply of men for you to prey on. Bob and vagene. If you're going to remain weaponized, can we at least use you to defraud Nigerians and Indians? Bring some money into the movement the right way, won't you?

When you impose your boobs on me, I think of how disgusting your farts must smell from your fad diet. Only easy women show the swell of their breasts to anyone with an Internet connection. Repent, e-girl!

Kings To Mentor

Hey, yo, King! I'm Confidence Huckster. Looking for kings to mentor right now, need like 5 of you guys to sign up for my private coaching group right now going to take you to the top. It's gonna cost you a lot of money but you're gonna see GAINZ and who doesn't like that. I am more well-versed in psychology than you are because I read a couple Carl Jung books and you're a dickweed because I purposely weed out people who are smarter than me by not taking their timely feedback so get in line, KING, I'm going to give your life the 180 Treatment. Like that? (Will Smith "haha" with chin flicking upwards movement). Just made that up because I'm on my hustle every day and you're not good enough until you've given me some money for some of my secret confidence tricks. It's not my natural, in-borne personality that I am dressing up with a little bit of intellectualization and selling as a philosophy. No, all of this shizzle right here I learned from the GRIND, my kings. You like that I say, "King"? Haha, learned that one from my own genius because the only person who influenced me is the mentors whose names I won't give to you because you'd just skip over me. And my daddy.

My daddy came to America with *nothing* to his name. Then he bulldogged his way to a nice real estate portfolio (never mind that American real estate was cheap as bricks in the 1970's). Now he's a King and I'm set to inherit all of it and now I want to show you the tricks and tips to real estate wealth like he did, once upon a time. My daddy did not hit me when I was a kid. No way! We're not talking about that. My father came to America for the *capitalism*, which I haven't talked about until the last two years when I quietly realized it was completely untenable for me to not be at least flaccidly sympathetic to conservatism without my business taking a huge hit cause people would figure out I'm a fraud and my children are quietly afraid of me because I'm too dominant. See, the secret is that wipipo, the race I proudly joined cause I hate my own, wipipo are *weak* because they don't have the jungle ferocity to fight and fornicate the banana mush out of everything they encounter. Low time preference? Who the CarlJung cares about that? Haha, see, there I get to cussing when I'm on my *grind*. Wipipo are weak and who gives a musclepump about having the historical and philosophical nuance to track down the origins of their problems and spur a true Middle America revolution when you can just act like a tough Gabriel-Marquez (like my daddy) and just *bulldog* these wipipo because they've become accustomed to getting run over by Third Worlders in public school. Just more of the same, baby. Every day a new hustle. It's all in the hustler's mindset but oops, Carl Jung. Deep psychology mastery. Masculinity. Mindset. Nootropics to cope with your anxiety because deep down you know you're defrauding people. Hey, they real estate portfolio is up. These kings out here taking care of their families. I'm doing all that. I'm good. I'm a good person. I'm not assuming a contrived black man's personality because "cool" is a psycho-social aberration resulting from managerial elite driven mass migration that doubles as ethnic cleansing and it's the only "American" personality I've ever known because my Jungian racial memories only go back to the jungle my parents crawled out of to participate in *capitalism*. Kings, stop overthinking things and hit the weight rack. When you hit the weight rack, I can dominate you because I have a LOUDER VOICE THAN YOU. Then you are distracted and I can extract resources from you while your mood improves and so you think I've given you something deep when you could get more help for yourself by listening to the material I'm sourcing my wizardry from while jumping rope and come to a deeper grasp of the concepts than I have because you have a higher IQ than me and your racial memories go back further than that of a shopping mall vagabond who got beasted up on supplements. Deep, vagal nerve breath. You have everything to learn from me and I, well, I am your *mentor*. Always have a *mentor, king*. Closing this segment out by staring intensely straight into the camera, into your soul.

Always Be Nice

Being mean doesn't get you anywhere! Always be nice. Repeat that five times. When you're mean, you disincentivize people from making better choices with their lives. There's no such thing as tough love because that's just emotional abuse that you haven't processed from your own childhood. In fact, not only should you never ever be mean, you should always be self-consciously happy. When you are meeting people in public, keep a smile on your face no matter what. Even if you are exhausted, bored by someone, or just overwhelmed with how much attention people are giving you because you are always nice all the time – you should not feel those things or even acknowledge them. Just keep smiling and self-consciously being your True Self. You are, after all, the most luminescent person to live since Ancient Times. Why? Because you read some of those books, of course. And because you help people. And so therefore why would you ever need to consciously acknowledge an unpleasant experience. You are purely philosophical and when unpleasant experiences flash up into your consciousness, you should grit your teeth visibly and look up and away before returning back to being the most self-consciously happy person who has ever lived.

Never be mean. Never show anger to anyone but an absolute Communist child-molester and only then do it in an overly dramatic, polished way that *conveys* a lesson. People deserve to see the real gritty stuff from you. Yeah, that's good. But then back off from being mean and get back to being the most amazing individual. If you don't, I will torment you with nightmares that you won't acknowledge to yourself because to share them publicly, which everything that has any emotional or philosophical juice to it should immediately be mined for content, would shine a light on how you are human and have problems and after all, that's not what philosophy, masculinity, saving the West, hustling for a business, or taking on mentees is about. Just keep smiling, you magnificent hero.

There Is No Fight

This isn't a fight. This is a business! We are going to business our way to victory. If anyone gets in our way permanently, we will just whine and complain and then get on with our lives. See, the trick to Draining The Swamp is to turn off the TV. Then the Swamp will drain itself! That's how it works. Alternative media wins the day. Millionaires and billionaires who lied the public into bloody war after bloody war will be the losers. They'll be on the outside and well, they'll just have to *change their business practices.* They won't have to give back that money they stole through fraud. They won't have that money forcibly taken from them by justice squads. No, when we tune them out – they lose! It's as simple as that. Hey everybody, don't listen to them. They're lying to you and I can prove it. Done. Now my business is even bigger than before. This is good. This is evidence I am winning.

When you tune them out, it helps you on an individual level. There, done. They lost! The marketplace of ideas won. Free speech for the win. Huzzah! We will never have to remove their right to vote or take away their citizenship or lock them up in cages for having blood on their hands because we'll simply just disengage from them.

That's enough. Consider yourself ostracized, statist! Now we can all live in peace in our covenant communities. This is ideal. And my business made a lot of money Draining The Swamp. That's great for the young people because now there aren't wars. There are still warmakers in retirement but hey, who cares about them. They're losers. I like to give them goofy nicknames like Trump does. We won!

Strategy Guide Moment #6

The 10 Best Sounds In The World

1. Bulldozers backing up all day long in newly-built subdivisions.
2. When women make music for the club.
3. Cities being razed in Total War.
4. Charlie Kirk saying, "Israel".
5. Female traffic judges adjusting their reading glasses to look down on you.
6. Aztecs death whistles when the pandemonium breaks out.
7. SWAT teams pulling up because of a joke you made.
8. Elizabeth Warren taking the lead in the 400m relay.
9. Costco disabling people so they look more convincing on the cover of their magazine (that's a joke).
10. Jeff Bezos cuddling up with his Latina gf

MAGA Hustler

Salutations, white people. I am a strong man. I live in a difficult neighborhood and I am proud of it. Now I am naming the phone area code of my neighborhood. This is my territory. I will yell in your face and sucker punch you if you disrespect my neighborhood. Just kidding. All that is behind me. I am a reformed brutalitarian. I found a higher calling when I watched a Leadership Summit from within the conservative ranks. I was inspired by the ferocious, revolutionary spirit that has taken hold of the ranks of the minorities in this nation. Now I am more honest and sincere.

My former life was difficult. Because of my lower IQ and innate tendencies toward physical violence, I developed a dark, unending nihilism that drove me to sell substances to people of your complexion. Sometimes I copulated with female children of your race younger than 18. I especially preferred the late high school girls of your race, which is different than my own. I deflowered many of these girls. My DNA is in their spinal cords somewhere, if the scientific rumors are to be believed. These substances I sold to your people, the only progenitors of civilization on the entire globe, contained trace elements of common household supplies. I did this to make a greater profit than the other businessmen in my neighborhood. Some people got sick from this admixture. Perhaps some died. I am not open to thinking about that, however, as I am a proud prophet of the new revolutionary spirit espoused by the businessmen of the race I made lots of money off of.

No, I am not interested in individually tracking down the people I victimized with my equatorial predations and apologizing to them each, adding considerable funds to their personal banking accounts as part of my restitution. That is not "aiding the mission" or "optical". Instead, I must be seen posing with my racial brothers by as many people as possible. We are revolutionary new businessmen who want less government, lower taxes, and some mild controls on immigration but we don't ever talk about that part because there are next to no pressures on us to do so. We are the future. We are very assertive about it. We are winning. If you oppose us, that's because you are a "hater" – to use some urban parlance. Excuse me. Sometimes my old life still slips in, here and there. Do not hate the revolutionary businessman, hate the nature of the competitive outing,.

Home Renovation Show

There's a pair of twin brothers. They are dressed like homosexuals. They are showing off an $860k house to a yuppie couple that has a supremely successful t-shirt printing business in California. They have three sons. Cute kids. The father looks like a dick-weasel, like he hasn't done something physically strenuous in a decade. His wife helps him with his business. There's a Chinese guy at the computer, helping design t-shirts. I see the t-shirts now. Jerk-off shirts. Probably got a contract with Zumiez or Pac-Sun. Those still exist, right? The *urbanites* haven't looted them completely, have they? The couple is wavering on the house. Obviously, this is a ploy by the producers and the house has already been purchased by the couple. I dislike being lied to so blatantly. If we were in a video game, I would frag whoever made this show. Video game violence! Now they have the house and they came under their 1.1 million dollar budget. Great! So, they're going to waste nearly $200k on renovations to make this place look less classical with columns and such to a more "modern" look of shiplap and industrial bullshit. This is so goddamn tedious. Why aren't they putting this money away for their children? Maybe they are and it's the show's budget that is covering the renovations.

Look, the homosexual twins are wearing fuchsia and magenta Express shirts, working on the renovations while wearing brand new, $80 gloves that don't have a speck of dust on them. Hardworking men! Now the woman is fretting over the living room. I want her to threaten to kill herself. Not in front of the kids, of course. Just in front of this weasel of a man she married and his homo twin friends and the producers. "I'm gonna kill myself!" she screams. Then they spend 2 minutes of airtime figuring out where they'll put the contraption she's going to hang herself from. Zero reaction from everyone around her…just an immediate need to spin this into some useful moment for the show. "Of course, let's tear out the fireplace and put a hangman's noose there using this FiberTex © rope we ordered from Home Depot." That's the real spirit of this tripe. They're all suicidal, chasing money so they can spike their blood sugar in more and more opulent private settings. They hate the kids but want the kids to be well-occupied so the parents can fry their coombrains on the Netflix home theater they installed where a piano room used to be. Should we just throw a bunch of weapons into the middle of the living room and they each have to rush in and then hack at each other in a bloody melee? Wouldn't they be more stimulated by that? Give it time. Hey, this is cynical, right?! They're *gentrifying*. They're raising their standard of living. This is the glory of the free market. Want to get rich selling your acquisitive personality to homosexual producers who will plaster your face all over supermarkets in Middle America? Who's to say no? They're just cynical and unfulfilled in their own lives. They can't get away from you but hey, that's not your fault.

Ah, a relief. I'm leaving the room the television is playing in. Just need to convince the people running this establishment that they shouldn't air this stuff even though explaining the *why* to them would take a long time and probably involve some kind of emotional enlightenment on their part that their slavish lifestyles won't allow for. There, I've done my part. Change happens at the individual level!

Climate-Anxiety Syndrome

These poor kids. At the doctor's office today and the goddamn BOARD BOOK that is specially meant for 1-2-year old's is talking about climate change. The Inner Chimpanzee rages, thrashing about in a berserker fury, smashing everything and killing other chimpanzees. Hole in the drywall! These kiddos get it everywhere they go. *Highlights*. Remember that magazine? In the 80's and 90's those things were plastered everywhere. What are they filled with now? Folktales from China. Little black boy and white girl pairings. Dogshit "poetry" from oppressed minorities. Ph.D. dickheads talking about space in a way that gets kids to feel estranged from themselves. No mention of Christ. Everywhere. These *Highlights* magazines are still everywhere. Poor kids.

The conservative press, what little of it exists, is talking about kids having "climate-anxiety syndrome". Psychologists in the EU are treating children as young as ten for this witchery. The APA calls it "Eco Anxiety". Millennium Kids found that 96% of kids aged 7 to 25 consider climate change to be a serious issue. Experts say that the children are having trouble processing the information, so it's up to parents and teachers to "provide hope" that there will be a solution. What doom and gloom. What a con job. My heart goes out to all these kids trapped by shitlib parents and teachers. Hey, Whole Foods and Amazon is raking in the millions on this voodoo. The government is quite sated. These kids are getting trained to become eco-terrorists and we're supposed to shut up and go along with it all. Inner Tiger attacks Inner Chimpanzee and blood spurts everywhere. This climate stuff is going to lead to babies being eaten. And it won't be liberal children that will be eaten. They'll use those Boston Dynamics robots to come steal your children on account of their carefully tracked carbon footprint.

STOP

Raise some animals. Read the books *our guys* are selling. Play a video game for a bit. Take a walk. Enjoy it. Breathe in deeply. Hit the gym. Wear a cowboy hat. Do like I.C.E. and trick some illegal Mexicans into jumping in the back of your truck. Gotcha! Feed bread to the ducks. Step in duck poop. Say 'hi' to the receptionist of your planned community. Enjoy a cheeseburger cooked in beef tallow. Do something nice like give a loved one a brief backrub. Get your head out of that space. They're demonic. They're devouring children. As sick as it is, it's a selective pressure. Help as many as you can and live well knowing you didn't participate in the death cult. Breathe again.

Traffic Escapades

Noticing that guy that pulled out in front of me and now I'm driving alongside. Banana yellow Jeep. California plates. Colorado University sticker on the back. Drives 10 miles under the speed limit. He's early 50's. Dressed in a 6-panel high profile cap (the ones with the flat brims that the drummer of Blink-182 wears) and a flannel shirt. Proceeds to go 15 miles under the speed limit when we get out onto the highway. Is he turning Montana purple? Is he sucking the life out of this place that reminds me, demographically, of the rural place my childhood once was? Does he out-earn me significantly? Does it make me toxically envious to see that the meager, subdivided lot he drove out of had a huge house on it and he's the only one living at it and clearly no livestock or vegetables grow there and it's just a place he watches TV inside of? Is it anti-human of me to wonder about this sort of thing aloud at several points in this book? There's something sick in him that sets him against what is beautiful in the world. When there's LESS GOVERNMENT, will he and I be less estranged from each other? Will I feel more benign toward his physiognomy and leave him be? Aren't I already letting him be and he's destroying everything that's left? When will his California money run out and the people love this place for more than just the Instagram likes are left stuck with some pine-stick craftsman mega house scarring up the landscape? I'm repeating myself. I'll get off of it.

Stop Fighting Retards

Bruh, stop with this fighting of retards. Stop cackling at your escapades. They aren't clever. They're merely brutish. You're not sticking the knife in like you think you are. You're squabbling with 85 IQ knucklcheads and getting your blood up. Our enemies are more sophisticated than that. They've gone to law school and shit. They could ruin you by recording just one of your outbursts. Bye-bye, decent life. Hello, infamy. Bro, just stop. You're not going to "retake the streets." You're thinking at a low level. Elevate yourself. I'm

not going to carry your ass. You either get in with the real
players or you send money to those who are. Nobody is
going to treat you like a king for squabbling with nobodies.
You can say it all in a look, anyway. Leave the idiots be.
Operate at the best level you can. Turn your fight into
something aspirational. Something grand. Something akin to
a life's struggle. Something like that. And always, always
reexamine yourself along the way. Nobody is immune from
rust. Dance the tightrope and do it right. Don't sling mud
with pigs. You are better than that. You are capable of more.
But I'm not going to carry you. Not one bit.

Most People

I have lived in many different countries, most
continents on the globe. I love interacting with people. Most
people are decent. Their politics are trash. That's it. Well,
and the pollution and the child abuse. There's those, too. But
it's not lost on me that I have pleasant interactions with most
people I encounter in the world, so long as they don't bring
their stodgy, cruddy politics into the situation. I wish I could
say that people are just "too overpoliticized these days".
That's such a cope. The truth is that my views are what the
common person in the USA believed in the 1870's. My views
are UNDERpoliticized compared to the average person in
the USA now, jamming their brains full of mass
entertainment, spiking the hell out of their blood sugar at
every juncture, dosing up on SSRI's, and getting their views

on government from washed-up Boomers. Something like that. I have the politics of a barnyard chicken. Or a frog, you could say. Simple. So simple. It's the massive unprogramming of propaganda I undertook. Any appearance of complexity comes from that. The truth is so simple. Muhammad Ali spoke about birds of a feather on a TV show. That's it. That's all it is.

People are pleasant, when they're flocking with their own feather. It's the race-crazy middle-aged women on wine and psychotropics that treat me like a Nazi. The humble Chinese veggie lady I bought my eggs from for seven months didn't give two spits. She was sweet to me without fail, though I am from a different flock. She knew it and I knew it. And her flock ran things. That was enough for us and we shared something wonderful for a time. She taught me most of the Mandarin I still know. But the middle-aged harlot at the store who gave up her own fertility to raise children from another flock (and she *was* fertile at one point), she treats me like I'm less than dirt – like I am a demon. She forgot her own humanity. She treats me like I forgot my own. But I have not. I suffer the lack of company. She is legion. My heart bursts with love and hope that others will get it. She scratches and claws and hisses.

Humans are not pets! I won't be a pet! I won't stand for it when these globalized people turn others into their pets, their mascots for causes. What Greta Thunberg's parents are doing to her is horrific. But it's everywhere now. People are leading their children to slaughter. They're in the overpoliticized state. You're willing to cut your kid's genitals off for your politics? You're willing to walk around in a murderous rage and hiss at a man who dares bench press and maintain some self-respect in the face of your insolence? It's in the air everywhere now. The murderous rage. It's not mine. The anti-whites want to kill. They want an open ethnic cleansing. If you're empathetic, you pick up on it. But most people can't handle it because they don't have the philosophical backing. You stick your head down in the sand, you join the "anti-fascists", or you freak out into your own personal life, causing a bunch of dramas. Murderous rage in the anticipation of Hell's advent is in the air. They're making it this way, the Pelosi's and such. The invaders. The elite.

The Chinese veggie lady isn't making it this way. She's with her own flock. The Filipina crispy roll lady selling her wares to Oregonians on Facebook *is* making it this way. She's invasive. She contributes. I don't offer comfort food and primitive sexuality. I offer the sense to see through the rage. I offer the kindness and goodness of a barnyard chicken, pecking about and clucking a tune. But the inverse must be made out of me. I must be made into the demon that the race-baiters and mascot-keepers are summoning. I won't accept it. I hum the simplest tune. Some of *the outsiders* would crucify me for it. I won't accept that.

People *love* me until they "learn" my politics. Rather, the conditioning they've been beaten upside the head with for generations kicks in. Then all perception of my interpersonal ease, my curiosity, my warmth and mirth – all of that disappears. *They* try to put me in the void of their own spiritual death. But I won't exist there. I am not willing. I will always put it back onto the evildoer. That is the right way. It's the only way. I exorcise the demons and for that I am demonized. I don't buy it. I won't be lied to. I won't suspend disbelief for the benefit of the doubt. You need to exorcize the demons, too. Or you will suffocate. Confess. Repent. Be born anew. That is the only way. Let go of the posture. Flow. Flow again.

Voter Suppression

One of the queerer wings of the shitlib coalition is the voter activism wing. Swaths of so-called journalists writing for major publications spend the large part of their energies fighting against "voter suppression" and bringing awareness to Democratic efforts at "voter enfranchisement". We all know that the Democrats gave up on the argument in the 1960's when they began wholesale importing the entire Third World. Their ideology is evil. Now they do everything they can to get evil-sympathetic people to vote. They target anyone who will drag standards further down. Was your home society a burning hellhole that never invented anything or resolved any civic issues since the dawn of humanity? You're the perfect candidate for enfranchisement. In fact, you are a victim and you should kill white man for his natural-borne preference of plumbing and Christianity.

Have you actually murdered someone? That's all in the past. Now you are aggrieved. Whitey is keeping you down. You should kill him. But not openly in streets. Just do it at the ballot box the way we tell you and the way you're inclined to since you're a murderer. When you murder white children at the ballot box, you are doing it with an air of legitimacy and therefore anything terse or unfriendly that is said to you or any measure of justice that bends back your way is actually just racism and you should burn down whole cities in response. We journalists will make a martyr out of you, our pop stars who are anally compromised will sing out on your behalf, and the producers and financiers who keep this whole thing going will pour millions into your legal defense. Anything to serve Satan!

I've noticed these journalists constantly prattle on and on and about "Republican efforts to suppress the vote". They put out unending "concerned" pieces about how Republicans are shuttering polling places on campuses. They do this because students, anyone under 35 really, vote overwhelming for the left. This is for a number of reasons, the primary one being demographic. America has been invaded by the Third World and white births are now being outpaced by the "minorities". Young people in America now are not part of a *nation*. They are here for the big money grab, just like the business and bureaucratic overclass that is importing them. Real Americans wear Nike! They buy Apple products, listen to Lizzo and Shawn Mendes, and they most def make fun of corny white people because *white people weak!* They are not beholden to the same "hate crime" statutes by the anti-white judiciary. They get the n-word pass, no problem. And because of Affirmative Action, every American institution has been forced at the point of a gun to give them preferential hiring status. The institutions are now so thoroughly politicized against whites that they throw themselves upon the tender mercies of the invading masses with reckless abandon. The young people are the most persuaded by all this. They haven't paid taxes, supported families, or had to develop any kind of low time preference on account of the massive *social safety net* that has existed since LBJ was flashing his cock to news reporters. And the majority of these youths come from broken societies that have never demonstrated a capacity for the kind of low time preferences that keep the West running. Yet, they are entitled to vote! The voting age is 18. That's prime drunk-driving age for Aztecs. That's prime cousin-molesting age for subcontinentals. That's prime smash-and-grab age of fatherless youths of a certain persuasion.

The journos at NY Times don't care about any of this. They want to see Hillary, Elizabeth Warren, or whoever else taking the reins of executive power in order to institute a true cosmopolitan bazar where corruption is the organizing force. This is the only path to extending and continuing their illegitimate influence and undue prestige. Their parents made a fortune swindling Middle America, they must continue this fortune by swindling the pliant, deranged New America. They're relentless, by the way. "Get Out The Vote" is their religion. They know that any direct counter-pressure against them is rhetorically suicidal. That's only because the

GOP has been run by autistic chamber of commerce potato brains like Canada's recent miserable failure, Andrew Scheer. Mitt Romney. Paul Ryan. The Bushes. To be initiated in GOP leadership, you have to have this same basic ethos: fuck America, grab the bag. So whenever one of these hapless dotards has stepped up against journo efforts to give rapists the vote, their lack of moral fiber is easily pointed out and ridiculed. The GOP has never thought to run candidates who aren't in on the lobbyist payola, ones that come from what's left of the middle class, ones who are willing to unironically "suppress" the vote and not play for media brownie points. Yes, rapists/murderers/illegal aliens/etc. don't get to vote ever. Fuck them! There are plenty of Americans who have the stones to say this, they just don't get anywhere near the halls of power because local GOP leadership gatekeeps anyone who has any verve. At the local level, the GOP is run by easily offended middle-aged soccer moms, local businessmen who figured out the grift, old-timers who are terrified of change, and increasing numbers of minority coalitions who want in on the grift for themselves.

The revolution that is coming will have to take a different path. It is unstoppable. You either try to understand it or you get in the way. There will be no cheeseball corporate stiffs running things in the future. They will be swept aside…in the kindest and gentlest manner ever, of course! The Boomers holding on to Social Security, their bloated pensions, and swaths of long ago affordable real estate will eventually die – despite milking Medicare and ruinously overtaxing medical facilities for the slightest of sniffles or

back aches. The young people who get it *now* have none of
the luxuries of the past. The playing field is tilted away from
them. A hostile media elite with *billions* in their coffers, AKA
an ability to play the game until kingdom-come and a public
schooling complex with a hard-on for transsexualism,
oppose these young people.

The power of social media, and it remains to be seen
if Big Tech suppression will prevail or not, is what allows
outsider candidates to primary shithead Congressmen until
they're so up against the ropes they bow out. Then the sea
change comes and we put in people who can limit voting to
taxpayers. That tilts America deep red since anyone who
pays taxes knows how badly the State and Federal
governments are screwing over value-producers. Social
media also allows for these journalist-activists to be
relentlessly "joked at". Always in a good-humored, good-
spirited way, of course! Believe it or not, shitlib journos have
terrific senses of humor and enjoy scrutiny.

Last of the Beatboxers

Do you know who is sexy? Rihanna. Interesting
name, huh? Rihanna "is a Barbadian singer, fashion designer,
actress, and businesswoman, who has been recognized for
embracing various musical styles and reinventing her image
throughout her career." She's a fashion designer! This is
important. Think of the good she has done in the world by

spreading her sexy message. Nothing sexier than when she twerks her poopy butt for the cameras. Damn, that's sexy! Let me see you poop, poop, poop, poop, poop! When Sir Edmund Hillary climbed Mt. Everest by himself, he was clad in Savage X Fenty lingerie and listening to Rihanna's "Take A Shit" single on his Beats.

When I am on the lam from African terrorist warlords roaming the lands of the Montanan Christian farmers that brought them over as cheap labor, I want to be hiding out in a cave listening to the sounds of Rihanna having sex with Jewish music moguls. But it must be set to a tasteful, sophisticated hip-hop beat. You may think I'm kidding, being facetious. The truth of it is, I openly celebrate Rihanna's fecundity. She reminds me of my Nigerian dwarf goat, who is in heat exactly 6x more often a year than my livestock that originates from Western Europe. Her gestation period is shorter, too. And my oh my, does she have a beautiful voice. She stands at the fence, wiggling her butt in the hopes that one of the sheep will mount her. She will bleat 15 to 18 hours in a row. It's a beautiful sound that fills the walls of my home. She poops some pearls on the ground and pushes her vagina up against the fence. The sheep try to mount her but they can't. Eventually she will start a lingerie line and visually satisfy the sheep. I stand out there while this is happening and I beatbox. I know my beatboxing needs work. Watching some tutorial videos later tonight. I need to support my goat in her efforts to stupefy and bewitch the sheep.

You think I'm kidding. You think I'm being racist. I genuinely do have a Nigerian dwarf goat. She displays the same mating ritual habits as Rihanna. The primitive parlance of her manner is much contrasted to the sheep in the other pasture. Many parallels! I celebrate her fecundity. I even beatbox to it. When I raised rabbits, I *proudly* placed New Zealand Whites in with Giant Angoras. When their mutant spawn would burst forth from the mother, escaping the savage jaws of the father, I would sit there at my electronic drum kit and play a backbeat while a local, talented youth poet would lay down verses. He would hang from the rafters of the barn with one hand, sing-songing into the microphone in his other hand. The rabbits were happy. My goat is happy. It's a happy farm.

But it won't always be this way. No, I must go on the lam soon from the Guatemalan narco-armies that prefer Rihanna's music. They would have sex with her in a heartbeat, you know. She is a very attractive woman. When I am on the lam, I will remember the good old days on my farm and how I helped my most fecund animals breed. That was their right, after all. No longer will I be able to stand in my barn in front of a projection screen, giving noble speeches to PowerPoints of the most important topics of the day. I will be reduced to living like a rat. It's not all that bad. You can have mud pancakes, if you want. I gave the *facts* when I did my PowerPoints. What people do with the facts, frankly I don't give a FLYING FRACK. I'm on the lam, remember? I'm reduced to beatboxing for crickets and the passing sparrow. Shh, I hear someone chattering outside my burrow hole I dug with my fingernails. I hear the sound of a machete being unsheathed. Now I am beatboxing. They are allayed. They know it's just the wildlife here. Spirits haunt these hills. All is well again.

Death With Dignity

I piss into a colostomy bag and my useless children sometimes call, except that one son of mine. I hate that guy. My lawyers are on the case! I learned a trick or two in my day about destroying families. I destroyed my own with the power of television and credit cards. Luckily, my important work as a Federal Employee was always there to pick up the slack whenever I would fly off the rails and verbally abuse my family late into the night while the television played. I am 80 pounds overweight.

I used to be more overweight but Uncle Sam stitched me right up. Stapled my stomach. I got on Jenny Craig. She helped me to lose weight. My mood improved for a while. Thank God for the disability checks. My family needed those except that son of mine. He's a junky! He started doing drugs in high school. My wife and I showed him that you have to say, "NO." No, we repeated to him over and over. It was tough love. Do what you have to do. Eventually we showed him that we have our limits and we cut him off from the second mortgage money I was dumping into his rehab. That freed up the money so I could rehab my lawn. It was looking awfully shabby there for a while. Those were lean years. Luckily, I was able to bring out the lawn experts. They set me up with a new underground irrigation system to replace the old one I put in when we moved here, where I am dying in my recliner. My son was dramatic about it. Tried to commit suicide, that piece of malarkey I can't stand because he distracts me from women's college softball. The lawn is much improved. I pour liquid gold on it. 24 carats. Then the grass is greener and golder. Read in one of my seven magazine subscriptions that you can pour beer on your lawn if the soil is too acidic. I bought a brew-from-home kit. It's in-style right now with the Gen Xer's, who I distrust because public school instilled in me a dislike toward people not of my age group. The second mortgage money nursed my brewery in the early stages until I had a large enough, well-tasting batch of ale to pour onto the lawn. Cost me $2200. I am laughing *very loudly* now so that you will be distracted and I will be distracted. I'm like a commercial.

Now, about that drug addict son of mine. I nurse secret thoughts of homicide toward him. I still have a few years before they take my driving privileges away from me. When he comes knocking on my door, telling me about how my generation ruined everything, I will back out of the driveway as fast as I can and ram into him like in the movies. He will die and there will be an exciting and interesting calamity around the place. My name will be in the newspapers. This is all a secret though. Outwardly, I am eager to vote for Obama's successor.

Halloween

This Halloween I am going to dress up as a consanguineous organized criminal and walk around my town, defecating on the sidewalk. The sheer momentum of the many exotic foreign dishes I will have consumed throughout the day using my food stamp money will power my ghoulish fun. I will join other men dressed as consanguineous organized criminals and we will rent a shabby brownstone. Forty of us will live there. Our next-door neighbors will be a family of three. We will loiter at all hours, chewing narcotic leaves popular in other parts of the world.

Halloween means there will be children around. We will leer at them to bring a spooky atmosphere to the festivities. There will be a considerable lack of consanguineous women in our area and so we will spend a lot of money on pornography. Pornography while chewing narcotic leaves is a must-try for any Halloween-goers. Once or twice and your brain's capacity for compassion drops out. Then you have what we usually call "The Hunger", but with approximately ten times more syllables to the word than is spoken in English.

Halloween night is an opportunity to walk to the little corner store one of our Spooky Guys owns whilst filled with The Hunger-slama-lama-ding-dong. Your bloodshot eyes and withering gait pair nicely with your emaciated Halloween physique and clammy hands. Your eyes stare out from the void of time and space, hungering for na-na. The police drive by and you spit out your narcotic leaves. On this particular Halloween night, there is a ghost whipping people at the ATM with a belt. Takes many Spooky Guys to subdue him. What fiendish fun! He is our competitor and we have him outnumbered. Now several of his ribs are broken. He doesn't care. He is filled with The Hunger-bwa-tah-ne-ne. We will have a blood vendetta with the inhabitants of his shabby brownstone before this is all through. My cousin, who is dressed as a hungry businessman, is sneaking grenades and automatic weapons into our local Ghoul Haunt. They shoot foam darts and explode into confetti. When we are made angry enough, we will pour out of our brownstone and play in the streets...much the same way some are engaging in water fights during Fourth of July. Halloween is different. We know Halloween best. This year will be the best one yet. We promise!

The Thirst

I am thirsty. The thirst is real. Why, oh why, mother? You left me when I was so little. Back into the workforce you went. I was a teensy baby. I needed to nurse for a year and a half. You gave me three months of your maternity leave and then back into the hive you went. I have been lost ever since. I am that age, always. I feel rage, all the time. I want to destroy everything. I want to become the Destroyer. You should have just held a funeral for me and pitched me into the dirt. That would have been more honest. Instead, you kept me alive with morsels of brainwashing disguised as love. You kept me going because to do otherwise would have brought the law down on our family. I don't want to bring the law down on me. I'm so thirsty. Just let me have my high-speed Internet connection and I will continue to consume the brainwashing disguised as love. I especially enjoy the ones where the women talking directly into the camera. When they speak to me, there's a hint of something in there that reminds me of what you did not give me, Mama.

Now I am all alone. The murderers are sending digital murder through my Internet connection. The intelligence services monitor me day and night. They will try to entrap me if I turn autistic. Then I'll be implicated in some bombmaking scheme. That will give them leverage over me. They'll take me to a remote training facility and give me lessons on how to shoot guns. They will break what little is left of me through repetitive imagery and recordings. Then their mind-experts will program sub-personalities into me, ones that have already been primed beforehand by the poison that was sent to me through my Internet connection. These subpersonalities will be highly competent at deadly things. Pedophiles movie directors who hang around these training facilities will make flops that depict highly stylized, distracting facsimiles of what I have been put through. They'll make the protagonist a sexy female so as to throw reasoning people off the scent. But not me, I am thirsty. I will be compelled toward *Her*. The Silicon Mama. When they're done turning me into a programmed executioner, they will set me loose with a bunch of funds. Every now and then my programming will call me back to some base of theirs somewhere in the underdeveloped world. I will be put through rituals where I behead Bedouins on film. I'll do it with a mask on and the rest of the world will think I'm not just some thirsty dude from Iowa.

If I'm this thirsty but 140 IQ or higher, there will be a different path for me. I will be recruited out of college through humiliation rituals at networking events. I will be funneled toward NGO's and success "camps" like the one Google holds every year. There I will be inundated with all the easy sex and PowerPoints on neo-liberalism I could possibly tolerate. Drugs that have been engineered in labs will be made readily available to me. Common street drugs will not. I will imbibe these drugs, have easy sex, and do my homework diligently. The homework will be easy because it's designed to be. The extra space where my intellectual curiosity once was will be obliterated by these engineered drugs. Sometimes they will make me take them in sensory deprivation chambers. Oh yes, I know some of this has already leaked out into the broader culture but *nobody* has access to the drugs that I do. To get those, to get into the bloodlust they foment, you have to be connected to the high powers. They dispense and distill. You have to hump your way to them. The old ones hump. All of them hump. You'd be surprised.

Good to write to you, mother. I'm all better now. I am sated.

Timidity

Sneaking around. Mother and father always treated me like a sneak. In the night I would slip out and commit my childish crimes. These were treated with terrible gravity. What agony for me. Now I am an adult and I work at a place I hate. I sneak around. Truly, I am one of the *Good Guys* but since I sneak around, I am made to feel like one of the *Bad Guys*. The bad guys keep pouring in. I detest them. I bicker with them over the coffee machine or the copying machine. This is my tiny rebellion. I don't have it in me to change. Are you kidding me? This is the honor code of the thief, "Once a sneak, always a sneak." That's my badge of pride.

I have clammy palms like the leaf-chewers. I am always nervous. I am hiding from you. This is my way. Part of my nervousness is laughter. I laugh at everything. It's not sincere. I force it to be. If you saw who I really am, you would scold me. I can't handle a scolding yet I induce it in anyone who ever gets close to me. Yes, stubborn that way. You won't get me to change. Instead, you will get fed up with me pushing you away like the thief that I am. Then you will eventually scold me and I will get to justify how you weren't a thief like me. Thief's honor code! Clammy palms from stealing things, naturally. We are a rare, noble breed. We are strategic and secretive. Our bedrooms are pigsties but only mistress thieves get to go in there. Off limits!

I'm still waiting for my mistress thief. She's out there, somewhere. Maybe she's a theater student. Maybe she likes to dress up at conventions. Maybe she will suck my peepee. Now I am laughing uncomfortably. Loudly, too. Controlling it. Have to stay quieter since I am a thief. But I do have a dagger. Little cuts, here and there. If you come too close, a little nick for you! I have homosexual fantasies because when my mother caught me masturbating and scolded me, I felt estranged from women and gravitated toward men. But men didn't like me and so I distanced myself from them like the thief that I am. Once they were at a distance, the idealization that I formerly held for them became sexualized because I can only feel aroused when people are at a distance from me. This is why even though I will choose a lovely mistress thief from a dress-up convention, she will have mannish tendencies and I will feel secure in her presence. That's the only kind of woman I'm interested in. Since most of these girls have monetized themselves to prey upon the loneliness of thieves, I will have to wait until I am older than 30 and some of them hit the wall and are willing to give a few years of their remaining fertility to me. Being the thief that I am, I will spend the early part of our relationship convincing her of the value of Nintendo. I will collect little figurines. She will give them pet names and talk to me in a baby voice when I feel upset. We won't show this to anyone. It will be between me and her. Thief's code! When we're at the end of her fertility window, we will have two or three miscarriages and then have one kid. I will name our kid an obscure name from a thief video game I like. Since there haven't been many good sneak type video games made, you can probably guess what we'll name our kid. We'll flirt with raising the kid the other gender, since my wife is somewhat gender-confused. When parent-teacher conferences eventually happen, I will wear pajamas and a hoodie to them. My kid and I will have a bunch of inside jokes. My thief-kid is such a goober. I'm a libertarian at heart.

Sandwich Line

We are all gathered at the banquet. I walk around on the grounds for a second and make sure everyone is accounted for. Two fellows show up carrying guns. It's good to see them. The making of the sandwiches is about to be announced and so I double step back to the gathering. I'm hungry.

The moment the sandwich bar is open, this little gal blasts past me. She's ravenous. She looks back at me to spite me. She had a brother. Or a sister. Or someone older than her growing up who she felt took the food out of her mouth. I won't deny her that. I am not that person. Not today, anyway. We aren't related. I know there wasn't enough for me growing up. She feels justified. I don't need to fight her. She's delighted that she bested me. To best a man like me is to please herself. It's an affirmation of her sincerest-held beliefs. That's the cover-up for the pain. I still want a sandwich. I'll give her berth. When she's done, since I am a threat apparently, I will fix myself one with pepperoni and provolone. Will she accept this? Will this be food out of her mouth? She's not fat. The food is only a small part of this whole mood. The speeding to the front of the line is the real mood. I've got the legs to do it every time. I'm tall! Oh, but she's tall too, you see. In her own way. She can provide. She's funny. She's intelligent. She's just as insightful as me. Those are the constant comparisons. When she can take the disappointment in herself no more, I will no longer be seen as tall. I will be killed off. No more sandwiches for me. Then she will find some other gathering. Personally, I want to walk around the place carrying a gun like my buddies, the baddies. But I'm too engaged to join them. The sandwiches mean little. It's the front of the line is what's coveted.

To Serve

If you concentrate all your energy on this man you have decided will save the world, sometimes he will give you a retweet. This will make your whole week and you will retweet him with ever renewed fury. He is rescuing you from your personal problems with that little bit of attention! Therefore, you must be singularly focused on him for years at a time. Anyone who expresses any kind of frustration with him clearly doesn't "get it" and must feel the lash of your bitter hatred – long stewing from the lack of your own personal efficacy because you'd rather live through social media and only do the things approved by your savior. You are a committed acolyte. He saved you from the lies of this world: religiosity, mass media, statism, being mean to other people, using fists instead of words. There are many other things he has saved you from.

Whoever he talks to, you instantly like for years and years. You don't care that the overwhelming majority of people he promotes are women. You know what masculinity is. Masculinity is what he says it is and whoever he talks to. Nobody outside of that. Anyone who is on the "outside" is one of three things:

1) A normie (those poor normies!)
2) A toxic abuser
3) Someone who is ignorant that must be brought in to the fold

You know how to save people but you'd prefer to support your savior doing it. You yourself don't want to do it. It took you 10 years to get over your own self-absorption in order to find a woman at the bottom of the looks rung. Never mind that intelligence and attractiveness are related. You only care about virtue. You are a virtuous man! Why? Because you retweet your savior and are not mean to people in-person, just overly pushy, self-consciously intense, and then withdrawing when your anger begins to overwhelm you. That's the masculine way to do things. Your middling maiden will never question this because she's just grateful to you, in all your splendid glory, that she gets to propagate the gene pool with her meek attributes. She's a real trad woman. A real throwback. Her consciousness will never expand to the point where she will realize how cringe you are and for that, she is the mother your children would have voted for if they'd had the choice. We should let all the beautiful women go to the douchebag alphas because we're intensely insecure in the face of the fact that many of them go hypergamous. Better to stay out of that whole tango, even if it means marrying a non-white woman. The tango has no tangible rules because the savior never laid out the rules in a presentation.

You don't need to actively fight in the culture war. Just retweet people who do. Don't find your own voice. Don't do it on an alt account. Just be a good family man who pays a little lip service to Christianity. Retweet your savior. That is good enough. Well done, wise man. You have lived from your deathbed back. No need to plunge your personality into uncertainty and strife out of a deeply dormant yearning to articulate and manifest. The savior already did that for you, even though he has never indicated that he has ever thought of things in those terms. You will pass this off as cynical and dismissive because the honest truth would shatter this whole façade you do twirling jumping-jacks to maintain every single day. Then you would be plunged into chaos because you didn't actually do things for yourself. You were like a remora on a whale shark, content to take whatever morsels came to you. Hey, it's philosophical! It's voluntary. The whale shark doesn't mind sycophants. You are a king, king. You made it to the next generation. Sit back. Do some retweeting. Agree with your Internet friends, some of whom you have seen in person, about the things the savior has said. Round and round you will agree. What a pleasant time. You are friends for life! And you are a *patriarch* now that you've found a semi-ugly woman to procreate with. Pat yourself on the back, my friend.

Migration

Yo, really enjoying this party of conservatives right now. This is such a philosophical depiction of the voluntary nature of interpersonal relationships. There's my black conservative friend, Andre. Andre is so sharp on his feet. He runs a successful podcast. You know the one where he's wearing a nice suit and has his arms crossed, looking up and smiling at the camera. He's a real pro. He's interviewed the best of the best. He's into guys who are into peak performance. I can relate to that. Besides, he's great with the ladies. I learn a bit from him here and there. He respects me because I'm always on my grind. We grind and hustle together. He's like a brother to me. Have you seen pictures of us on social media together? This is the glory of voluntarism in action. We share the same values.

Andre has a loud voice. I ignore how loud it can get sometimes and think to myself how grateful I am for this relationship with a successful black man. There aren't many good depictions of them in the media, you know? Did you know that 1/3 of all adult black men in America have been incarcerated at some point in their lives? We're changing all that. He with his podcast and me with my burgeoning platform. I've got some mega donors coming along with what I've got planned next. These guys are deca-millionaires. I shouldn't say but hey, I've got a little bit of alcohol in me. Like 6 beers. It's no big deal. There's Andre's voice. He's so funny. The more I drink, the less sensitive I am to his voice. Oh, the party's heating up now! Someone brought in a stereo system. Andre's hooking up his phone to it. Damn, he's got some good taste in music. He likes Christian music, like me. I love those beats. He's got it cranked up real loud how he likes it. What? I'm sorry. Can't hear you. I'm really caught up in the vibe right now. Let's talk out on the back stoop where all of my voluntary friends who share my values are vaping in order to nurse themselves off of cigarette addictions.

Ah, glad we are here now. You were saying? Yes, but are you aware that their unemployment rates are at an all-time low? No, he doesn't mind when I'm smooth like he is. In fact, he prefers it. I put just a lil' slang in there sometimes. See how I did that? You can do it, too. He'll like you more if you do it. If you don't, he will withdraw attention and affection from you. Only a little bit, but over time you will feel the sting. Trust me, you need him. He's successful. He recently interviewed the founder of Feeblebook. Yeah, I know that guy's a super liberal but Andre and him are cool. They go way back. Let's go back into the party.

What? Talk loudly into my ear and then I will hear you. Yes, I noticed. Those are his friends. They are proud black men like him. It's fantastic. Look how they clasp their fists and show steely eyes for the picture she's taking. They are masculine. We haven't been permitted to be that way for a long time now. They are closer to their natures, in a sense. I'm not supposed to talk that way. Give me another beer, please. Thank you. She opened it with her teeth? That's voluntary. We are all young and having fun. Oh, here come a few prouder black men. I'm noticing they aren't wearing shirts and ties. I thought this was a shirt-and-tie event. Let me go talk to this one man with a cigar tucked behind his ear. It seems he doesn't want to respond to me. That's okay, he's friends of Andre's friends. This is all voluntary. The music is *really* loud now. Ah, amazing! Look at all this dancing that is happening. Oops, she spilled her drink. That's okay, the new guys brought a lot of alcohol with them. Let's go back out on the stoop where my most excellent friends are now discussing the glories of peaceful parenting.

This is nice, huh? Them in there, partying with such enthusiasm and Andre getting pictures with everyone. Us out here, having fruitful philosophical conversations that if we recorded on a podcast would change the world. I am so relieved to see that Hans over there has nursed himself off of vaping. We are recovering! Could you ask that one fellow with the jersey on if he would shut the door? The music is getting hard to hear over. Everyone is welcome, don't get me wrong. It's just that we want a more peaceful, conversation-based area over here. That's how we planned it before the party started. He doesn't want to shut the door? I feel scared and the thought is that this man doesn't understand what we're trying to accomplish with this party for influencers. That's the thought. That's the only thought. I'm being honest and philosophical. See, I am self-consciously happy. Everyone knows it's me! I'll go talk to this man, despite my fear and because I'm courageous. You there, my brutha' (like that flourish?), could you please understand that we have shared values and that though you have a preference for loud sounds, I have an even stronger preference for quiet out here on the stoop. I'm sure you understand. We are all here voluntarily and I am choosing to not hear your music. Oh, my god! You are showing your teeth to me in a dangerous grin I have only seen in the movies. This is most troubling to me. This is no longer a voluntary interaction. Now it is time for me to go speak with Andre.

Hello, Andre. I'll yell louder into your ear. Good, now you can hear me. Say, Andre, there's a large fellow with a grimace on his face out back that is holding the door open. The music is spilling out into where we are discussing how women need to learn the hard facts about society and how they will toughen up and help us in our quest to make civilization great as it once was. You say this man is from your neighborhood? You're bringing him along intellectually and having patience with him as he absorbs the ideals of liberty and personal freedom? That is so understandable. I was once a statist. He's not a statist, you say? Oh, my apologies. He's already learned economics from Adam Smith. Gosh, I feel embarrassed that I was so assuming. I don't understand where that assumption comes from and I will drink a lot of coffee tomorrow so as to not reflect further on where it comes from. If you say he is one of us, I trust you. The grimace I saw on his face was probably just the look of curiosity as he could hear the conversations we were having about peaceful parenting. What's his Twitter handle? I will retweet him in a show of good faith. When I meet new people, I like to treat them the way they treat me. I treat them extremely well and when they don't treat me as well as I treat them, because they haven't done the personal work I have done, I treat them the way they have treated me. You, Andre, have treated me so well thus far. I trust that though the night may be kind of ruined, we will soon all be together on the back stoop discussing the concepts that will lead to our communal salvation. We have so much in common!

The Family Feel

Everyone wants the family feel back. The problem arises when there are too many cooks in the kitchen. A guys says to himself, "I am the most competent person I know in my tiny circle of relations and so therefore I am prepared to make the most glorious social media platform of all and I will assume anyone who takes issue with me just isn't walking in the light like I am." That's one too many cooks in the kitchen. Another will say to himself, "Though I frittered away my 20's and 30's contributing nothing other than the near-accident that I happened to reproduce before Trump became President, suddenly I am prepared to give extensive lectures on Western Civilization on my YouTube channel."

That's another cook in the kitchen. There's the woman who says, "Wow, when I post pictures of myself dressed in a way that turns on men, they give me attention for the strength of my ideas. Time for me to signal boost with any beta with over 500k subs." If she'd stick to cooking, she'd be invited…to watch the chefs cook.

Sometimes you just have to shut the fuck up. When you want the *family feel*, sometimes you're quiet. Stop clogging up things for people more competent than you by opening your flapper every time you have a thought. Distill it into something. Craft something. Concentrate on something difficult and endeavor. Work on the dimensions of your shitposting. Make something. A family that never shuts the fuck up is a family that is stressed and in need of validation. Men on our side convince themselves this is "thoroughly engaging!" when a lot of the time it's just cringeposting irl.

We all want the *family feel* back. We want the warmth of men in charge and women back in their orbits. The fashion went to shit. The architecture went to shit. On and on we could go. The talking? That's getting sorted out. You may be less of a leader in this regard than you think. Do you have another competency? Be a based plumber. I have a whole career that I just barely mention on the Internet. I know when things are better off private, building and growing into something wonderful. Stop mining every moment of your life for something to yap about. Put the words *into* something. Imagine a war room where all the upper brass never shut the fuck up cause each of them thinks he's the cock of the walk. Or the officers have the wrong man pegged as leader and he doddles and totters while the enemy gains ground. That guy needs to shut the fuck up sometimes. Getting attention doesn't grant your ideas merit. Sure, you get attention for the merit of your ideas but only up to a certain point. Otherwise, whoever was most right would be the top celebrity for however long. That would even be a mostly functional path for a *non*-multicultural society.

There's an old barbershop saying, and I'm going to butcher it, that says, "You learn when you listen and you ain't listening when your mouth is flapping." You learn when you listen. But if you are determined to fill other people's thoughts with your own thoughts at all time, you are not being "alpha". You are being a nuisance and you should shut the fuck up. There's no lack of "content" in the world. People flapping their gums. A lot of it is good. What a liberation that we get to speak to each other. Many wars already averted. Many crimes abated. This is a whitepilling direction we're headed in. The listening and *doing* is sometimes not there. We'll just have to nudge those people to the side, won't we? We're not talking about castigation and ruination of those clogging things up. We're talking about adjustments so there's better flow from the top to the bottom.

Right now, there are a lot of people doing the equivalent of putting people through their family vacation slideshows. We're trying to break the constraints and they're doing the equivalent of running around Mass, saying 'peace be with you' to as many people as possible in the hopes that they will be noticed and affirmed for being friendly. And if only the religious component was there. It's like a messed up public high school version of it. Some guys know the high school nature of social media and simply prey on people's pre-programming in order to vault themselves forward. Fuck those people. They fancy themselves sophisticates who can slide in with the cool kids in Silicon Valley, if it so pleases them. No, we have to break all of this and nudge or shove the people who are in the way. The people who lack this awareness. It's not like high school. It never was. That's psychosis. If they can experience it thusly, they will stop posting their boring family vacations on social media. Get out of the way. The family feel has nothing to do with vacations, the pathetic conceptions that bring these people comfort because they've been nursing addictions for years while comfortably snoozing in the maw of a murdering shark leviathan.

These people. They're just *relieved* to have a voice. "I have a platform!" they say. Then they clog it up with shit and invite any mouth-breathing person on just to get some *traction* (notice me for being good!). It's just a *relief* to get some attention and if you can be seen as good in the process, wow, you are A Keeper of Western Civilization. Give us a break. We're set against the entire industrialized world and you are nursing your wounded ego with one more middling post about how people, who don't love you, are scoring zingers? Stop making a spectacle out of yourself. Stop clogging things up and acting so butt hurt when someone doesn't want to go along with it. "We're all going to make it, kings!" No, we're not all going to make it. Stop lying to yourself and pulling others down with you and pretending you're doing the entire opposite.

Minority Report

You know what's conservative and free thinking? Being a non-white "free thinker" who mates with white women, thereby depopulating and deracinating the white people who built the society you "hustle" in. Let's "speak into existence" the decimation of the white race by deliberately avoiding advocating for any political positions that would allow the white race a reprieve from the senseless, lustful onslaught and suicidality currently tormenting it. I'm a proud black man! My parents moved from Africa to escape being slaughtered for having 110 IQ's. We lived in Europe where everyone treated us like gods. Now we have emigrated to America and we've joined *The Hustle*. It's a fun movie where we acquire as much as possible and only *slightly* raise the violent crime rates compared to the native population, though the IQ of our children will eventually revert back to the norm. In the meanwhile, let's strut around like the stars of this movie. Let's acquire as much clout as possible because a proud black man blows the minds of *white* liberals (not Jewish liberals because we're not supposed to mention that race or suddenly the collabs we've been getting handed to us like candy will dry up). Now that we're hustling in America, let's use Internet research to figure out where those "white liberals" are fleeing to. We'll track them down and then buy property near them like the kings we are. We'll be their neighbors and enjoy all the benefits and access that they do because that's what freedom is all about. Let me tell you the five things my platform is all about:

1. Always hustling and grinding
2. Abundance mindset, yo
3. Collabs with "free thinkers", especially the white ones with a lot of clout
4. Capitalism
5. Fucking white women and flying into a murderous rage and whipping up as much hysteria as possible against anyone who objects to this

I moved to America for *freedom* and tha *hustle*, so naturally I am not moving to *white liberal* cities like Atlanta, Baltimore, Detroit, or St. Louis. No, I'm a king. I'm aware that the "white liberals" are fleeing to pockets of Wyoming, Montana, Colorado, and Idaho. It just so happens that I had a free-thinking vision that told me that the set of my next music video is where they live. I'm gonna go there with my fast twitch muscle fibers and genetically lowered body-fat and show them all how lifting weights can temporarily improve their moods and distract them from how a huge portion of their kind are suicidal and troubled by the Leviathan devouring them. My solution? Lift weights and never say anything that a cognitive behavioral therapist is trained to see as "negative". Mood boosts and spreading my king seed.

What's that? You want me to solve the problems of my own people. Well, of course I'm doing that by buying up more of the land that your kids would have bought if the country hadn't been flooded by invaders for the past generation. You want me to go to people who are like me and confront them and you'll help me a bit? No, I am a conservative free-thinker who has tweeted milquetoast non-positions on immigration on five separate occasions (which is enough to fool the cornball retard whites who fill my coffers because they were raised to worship Will Smith as their planet savior). I don't actually want to fix anything for white people, I want to milk the crony-capitalistic system they built up after getting messed up on world wars they were misled into and central banking. I'm here to lift weights and rap! I'm speaking into existence my utter subjugation of the white race and their absolute adoration of me for doing so, so their pain is finally ended. You understand, right, dog?

No, don't go there you white liberal racist. I'm not going to back to the continent where the majority of my kind would murder me for having a 95+ IQ and imposing order upon them even though they'd accept it if we put into place a bunch of reforms that included increased access to iodine. Nah, I'm a skier. Look at me, I'm an alpine skier. I am skiing in this music video and saying many verses with filler words but you believe it to be deeply soulful. I'm going to have sex with as many white liberal women as possible who are drawn to me because their fathers were absolute failures in inoculating them with modesty and piety. I'm going to breed them out and you're going to thank me. And if you say anything against me, I'll simply pretend you don't exist for the rest of my life. If you come at me like brap-brap-brap, I've been done killed so many times and I'm still here.

This is the part of my monologue where I am not going to tell you how I and nobody of my tribe share your existential angst because we will be ascendant for the next 80 years off of the sheer momentum of all the aid you sent us. My tribesmen and I have a swagger that we are happy to make you envious of. We are *loud*. We do not acknowledge IQ differences. We do not acknowledge the demographic cliff. We don't have to. The future is ours. When we say of ourselves we are the greatest of all time, we neglect to mention that this is a condition of our tendency not to pursue careers as historians. Everything is NOW because that's essentially how we are hardwired. Our hierarchy is based on the loudest warrior who can plug the most people assertively into the moment. Combine this with some measure of intelligence and suddenly we have bewitched your entire, World War-sickened culture. You have the monumental task of peeling back layers and layers of blood to reclaim your astonishing, unprecedented rise in IQ. My tribe is the direct beneficiary of this and so I will be friendly to you but I always place my people first. It's abundantly clear in the way I speak to you. But I will not lead you back to yourself because that is none of my concern nor should it be. You have done it to yourselves and until you are strong enough, en masse, to reject someone like me – I will be here. I will encroach further and further upon you and I will enjoy it. I am not grateful because I am a self-made man, of course.

No, it's not a matter of being born in unique, temporal circumstances. My tribe won't undergo the same kind of mortal angst yours has undergone because we are mostly only capable of stochastic violence. Besides, we've got the food thing down as we have convinced you to feed us. We'll feed ourselves but it won't be enough. No, there will be no primordial dread that overcomes us by the turn of the next century. Anyone who infers this is simply a hater who I will refuse to acknowledge for the rest of my life. I am here to fight for my place at the table and if you resist the ideological temptation of an abundance mindset, you will be my mortal enemy that I will overcome with "my shine". Never mind you that biologists have been postulating and confirming for centuries that physical environments have carrying capacities. The West is underpopulated and I have come here to fill it with my seed.

Throughout the course of this entire monologue I have made references to my tribe but the truth is that I am a free-thinking individualist. The ideas that I am bringing to bear my force of personality upon and that I will bring to life with force when this unique, temporal social and psychology opportunity affords me the influence and power to come rule over you, are completely and totally the reflection of the individual. I am that individual. I only speak for myself. By saying this, I am distracting you from the fact that my tribe specifically will benefit from this ethos and the resulting governmental changes. You are supposed to look the other way because *you are weak*. I am ascendant, my people are ascendant. Any objection you have has no philosophical basis whatsoever. Watch how I perform persuasion on you, over and over, and you are forced to cede ground because if you don't you will become irrelevant. I hold all the keys. I am in the driver's seat. Your kind is *weak*. I am taking possession of them, especially the women. You are defeated. Since I have no limits, I will not be bound by your artificial "sporting" mentality. To me, everything reverts back to the sun and the sun burns everything in its path. You could say I am vitalistic but I have never framed things in those terms and I would never care to. The history is past. The history does not matter. You in your sentimental yearning. You will never fulfill your past. I am the now. I am the greatest of all time because my conception of time is different than yours. Now I am here. I am defeating you at every step. You notice how I am making it up as I go along? You must emulate me or you will be driven aside. Nobody is coming for you. I have taken over everything. I will not ask.

You cannot indict me so long as I keep this message inspirational. You have no legitimate defenses.

Navel

Hello, I come from shithole. My words are simple. I am a prophet. Silicon Valley made me rich. Thank you, H1B visa. Now I am wise on social media. Brief sentences. Joe Rogan supports me. 150 IQ. We win all the spelling bees. I am upper caste. I want to rule America. The wiser you are, the simpler your sentences are. The more I learn, the less I know. Profound, isn't it? But to me it is not profound. It is quiet. I meditate every day. My parents used one hand for wiping, the other for eating. I am your boss now. Many teachings, I have. I teach you about efficiency. I teach you about simplicity. I teach you quiet mind. My acolytes trip on micro-LSD doses. That was a long sentence. Calming the mind now. I am worth $200 million. Thank you, San Francisco. The left and the right are wings of the same bird. I am neither right wing or left wing. That is unwise. I am simplicity. Everything serene. The wiser I am, the quieter my mind is. You will learn this. You are not as far along as me.

Religion is a sham. The truth is universal. There are pieces of it in every religion. There is only stillness. San Francisco bleeds money into my coffers. I am benevolent and simple. My 147 IQ brother is, too. But he has not been on Joe Rogan yet. He is simple. Upper caste. America is ours now because it is for sale. We own large real estate portfolios. We are not American because that is an identity. No identities. Only simplicity and calm. You don't need drugs, only minimalism. We quietly urge congress to hire more people from shithole. We do it when you aren't looking. Simple mind, simple thoughts. We hire shitholers preferentially. Calm your mind. Breathe deeply like Wim Hoff, one of your great teachers. I am one of the five wisest people alive. Simple tweets. White men with shaved heads retweet me. They wear Peruvian beads. They do DMT but I don't. I am too wise. I say nothing when they do because we are all nothing. Religion is nothing. There is only the breath. I own three

Teslas. They have customized, simple layouts. Gaze into your navel, my pupil. The answers are there, in the navel. Now I am your landlord. Now my children are among yours. They will teach your children the quiet way. Quiet mind is wise mind. Child's mindset. Always learning. Spelling bee championships. Crypto currencies and Burning Man. I am the Happy Wanderer. In the quietest moments, my blood memories tell me to wipe with one hand and eat with the other. Now you know the secret of life.

Melancholy

You are never to express melancholy. That is born out of childhood trauma and besides, if you express anything approaching sadness – you will be harangued endlessly by the encroaching hordes. They will use the English we taught them to mercilessly tyrannize you for expressing a concept that has only ever existed to them when the village cow or a street dog died. Melancholy is the gemstone born from the strata of civilizational accrual. Melancholy has to do with the reflection upon the mythic, the sacramental, and the personal. Before the Wars, America was run by the melancholic. It has been en vogue since the 1970's to call them "Old Money". While this term is only a brutal approximation, the very fact that it approximates means that at some point a popular music act will be chartered bearing the term as its name in order to obfuscate its meaning further.

Never consider that the leisure time Europeans had together in communal lodges was what the first industrialized peoples approximated and established *instinctually* the moment they had patrician wealth. Never consider that they were well on their way to establishing this for everyone around them until piece of pie non-melancholics in the government loosened immigration controls and let in all the drunkards, gypsies, and wanton money-spenders the economy would support. Never mind this has happened three or four more times since, each of these waves pushing further back what could have been. Don't reflect on that because then you might feel things that no free-thinker would dare allow you to think.

Pick-Up A Woman

You walk up to her. Then you punch her in the face. She screams for help. Your Sharia Patrol brothers do as the imam said and grab her by the legs and arms from behind. Now you pick her up. She is struggling but you hit her a few more times until she is dazed. Then you take her to a van and tie her up. Gag her with a sock but not before trying to kiss her. She will spit in your face, just like in the movies. Now you have her.

You take her to a shabby basement where hundreds of men will cycle through. They will have sex with her while you keep her on low quality heroine. Her life will be absolutely destroyed but that's what she gets for wearing a short skirt out at night by herself. When she is ruined enough, you will begin to develop an affinity for her. This will happen during your lookout shifts where you sit on a folding chair with a large kitchen knife in your hand, making sure no women escape what has become an underground dungeon. You'll sneak glances at her. She reminds you of the war-torn hellhole you come from. You think if you could just help her a little, she'd feel better and see you as a kind of rescuer. You feed her extra rations and only put half the heroine dose into her when you're on watch. You're a peon and soon enough a man who is more experienced than you catches on to what is going on. He tells you something about this thing you're doing is religiously forbidden and this woman is the outsider. Something along these lines.

You sober up. You pick-up more women. You make more money. The fathers of these "women" even come and bang on the metal doors of the house your financier owns through a shell corporation that eventually connects to people who owner much larger buildings within the City of London itself. The fathers are arrested for disturbing the peace. People who look like them come and put them in handcuffs. The neighborhood is upset but you get to operate with impunity because in this country the genocide is openly accepted. Any major politician who declares otherwise is made to fear for their lives and their children's lives. They are met with constant bomb threats, deaths of pets, stuff like that. Your patrol brothers do some of the dirty work. You all feel good about what's going on. Reformers are chased out of the country. There are exceedingly few of them anyway and you'd kill them if they ever stepped foot here.

White Liberals

You know who is to blame for everything bad that ever happened to black people and minorities in general? *White* liberals. Yes, they are the scum of the earth. The majority of them owned slaves before slavery was abolished in America. They also funded the SPLC and ACLU that we used to love and celebrate but now hate because white liberals engineered how we thought back then. They took over all of the major newspapers, publishing houses, television networks, and organized sports and put deliberate programming into them to make us slaves on the Democratic plantation. Go back a generation before all that and remember it was the white liberals who met on Jekyll Island (am I really about to go Alex Jones levels here?). These crusty old white liberals met in secret and laid out the plans for the Federal Reserve Bank. Then they got another white liberal, Woodrow Wilson, and sitting members of Congress (who were all white liberals under the influence and extortion of other white liberals) to pass the Fed into existence.

You know who else was a white liberal? Yeah, not even going to say his name in these pages because he should be wiped from the history books.

White liberals are our enemy. They are white. We've had enough of the white media, the white press, the white banks, the white landowners, the white propagandists, the white financiers, the white lawyers, it goes on and on. White liberal. When all of the white liberals are gone, and we're not going to talk about how, then our people will be free.

Nobody gets to tell me how I should vote based on the color of my skin. I don't want to realize that it's the "should" piece of that equation that makes it a clever rhetorical device for me and that I am constantly espousing consciousness for my own tribe and creating an outgroup out of the white liberals. If you think into it, every race *should* vote for less government candidates because the government right now is in the habit of fomenting race war and enslaving everyone, white liberals included. Yes, those white liberals. They the devil. They're *white*. Special emphasis on their whiteness, in case you haven't noticed. But come on, let's not focus on identity even though I never posit things in terms of statism or minarchism because it's easier to single out a subsection of white people, given that white people don't riot in the streets when any of their kind are under duress. I'm not here to divide people. I'm uniting them!

Lies My Teacher Told Me

There was this social studies teacher of mine in high school that led an interesting life. He was a state college graduate from down the road. He had an unusual attitude toward me. I dropped out of the pre-AP and AP path because I was sick of the busy work they put on the intelligent kids. I realized that the sum effect of being completely doused in propaganda was that your critical thinking ability would eventually be cut off. I chose to be in the "regular" kids' class. He saw this and accepted it. He proceeded to allow me to lead long swaths of class time by allowing me to ask questions you weren't allowed to ask and to petition for certain movies and certain passages in the older history books to be covered. He was happy to do this because he allowed me to be what I was, smarter than him. We were in an intellectual colony together. He with the official title of magistrate and I, with my on-the-ground stewardship. We had a delightful amount of fun in the two semesters we were together. He knew things about history he wouldn't let on to anyone at work because it would compromise this comfortable life and salary he had established for himself. Instead, he would give a knowing smile. Those smiles were electric. They broke the matrix. A few other kids eventually caught on to what was going on and word got to the department chair. The department chair also had the knowing smile and let me lead, at times, when I moved on to his class. But he had a family to feed and kept it much closer to the chest. The majority of the kids in my class simply laughed at what they thought were my "antics". The third and final social studies/history teacher was an old timer, born in the late 1930's. He allowed me to do my thing in the one class of his I took. He took a lot of sick leave that term so I didn't see much of him, a shame.

I managed to wrangle two courses over my last two years of high school with the Vietnam vet teacher who openly talked about his war stories and how he owned stake in a bar. I was the only one to probe him on this stuff. He knew what I was up to. He had endless JFK conspiracy theory books on his back wall. This was with the advanced kids, these classes. My classmates regarded me as a funny oddity, asking the questions I did. There was a line. With all of these male teachers I had, there was a line I could not cross. My intellectual curiosity could not stray beyond it. They indicated this to me, each in their own way. The old timer was the crotchetiest about it. The young state college grad was the funniest about it. The Vietnam vet was the *realest* about it. He helped set me free, in a sense. My classmates never seemed to catch on. I was always frustrated by that. I took comfort in the observation that only rarely did they seem strained by my questions.

I tried this tack with other teachers of other subjects but it was only the history/social studies guys who gave any ground. I wonder if Zoomers have an entirely more explicit but similar experience to what I went through. I felt alone in it, back then. I hope some of my high school classmates write me eventually and tell me that they got it then or that they get it now.

Forgiveness Culture

I've stayed out of it because I'm focused on philosophy and America First but it looks like "cancel culture" is about being "cancelled" for things you said or did in the past. Roseanne had her show cancelled for being pro-Trump and then making a joke about how Valerie Jarrett looks like the Planet of the Apes character (and she does). Dave Chappelle made light of cancel culture in his latest special, talking about how any little thing you said in the past will be used against you. He talked about Kevin Hart making jokes about homosexuals on Twitter nearly a decade ago and losing his Oscars hosting gig on account of those tweets being dug up. This is my understanding of Cancel Culture.

The left is unrelentingly unforgiving. All this does is box you in and paralyze you. You are paralyzed into their doctrine. It's self-reinforcing. You may say to me, "Steve, over the course of this book and on social media you speak in a condemnatory way. You have your mind made up about whole groups of people!" The thing is, my mind is open to changing if I see evidence that something has changed. The job of a philosopher is to describe things as they are. The job of an artist or "consultant" (which I loosely term my business practice) is to describe what could be. I have tremendous hope. I hold the hope for people out in the world, despite disliking their behaviors and being constantly dissatisfied with less than near-total competency. I also know you adjust by IQ. Smarter people are just capable of more. The same principle works for beautiful people. I didn't make the rules. Don't think I don't feel envious of beautiful people sometimes.

Forgiveness comes from understanding. When you understand why you did what you did, then you can make real amends by reaching who you wronged and by correcting your own behavior. Your feelings usually let you know when you've done wrong, that's why the left is so into emotional propaganda. They want to reprogram your natural sense of justice to fit their paralyzing world vision. I don't want this for you or for anyone else. When you think to yourself that I have been unfair or inaccurate with someone or something, first it's probably best to wonder if you're being an emotional globalist about it. Second, it's useful to understand that a knowledge of ethnocentric strategies (which sans universalism inevitably come at the expense of another group), natural gender roles, demographics, and intelligence research can set people free. If you know your shortcomings and the shortcomings of others, you can operate with more understanding. You can bring yourself to a state of forgiveness and help others to get there, too. Quite frankly, groups that have been far and away more violent to other groups (in THIS lifetime) should be understanding their violent natures and making amends with the aggrieved. This is just barely starting to take place and it remains to be seen if it will become an overarching trend. With the self-forgiveness, in terms of groups, comes the resolution to become less corruptible and less persuaded by shortcuts.

Would you prefer I never said what was said in this book? Not going to happen and only if you're a *white liberal.* I will find a way, no matter what. You will not silence me. And I will not be blotted out by less articulated, less accurate voices. Still, we are here to learn together and to improve the standing of TRUTH in the world. Put God first before yourself and you will overflow with understanding, amends, and forgiveness. Then your world is righted. Put *yourself* first and watch yourself become paralyzed and globalist.

You think I acted out in this book? Thank your lucky stars these words are making it to print instead of being repressed. We need open dialogue. This is my contribution. Don't think for a second I didn't point out shortcomings of my own kind. Minority, ethnic chauvinists have printed the most vile, untrue nonsense ever but they're enshrined because they contribute to the ever-creeping paralysis. A dude who keeps a flock of sheep, does carpentry on the regular, and never raises his voice or hand at his children writes about the madness of the paralysis and he's pilloried for it? Not anymore. Enough is enough.

Made in the USA
Middletown, DE
06 December 2019